Savoring Sephardic Cuisine: 101 Delectable Recipes

Fireside Feast Grill

Copyright © 2023 Fireside Feast Grill
All rights reserved.

:

Contents

3

INTRODUCTION

Savoring Sephardic Cuisine: 101 Delectable Recipes is an exciting new cookbook that invites readers to explore the culinary delights of the vibrant Sephardic Jewish culture. This book contains recipes from around the world, spanning Jewish communities in Spain, North Africa, the Middle East, and the Americas. Over the centuries, these communities have taken their favorite ingredients and transformed them into flavorful, memorable dishes. Through the pages of Savoring Sephardic Cuisine, readers will discover the secrets and techniques used to make these famous dishes, while learning about the customs of their Sephardic ancestors.

The recipes in this cookbook use ingredients from around the world including fruits, vegetables, grains, legumes, nuts, dairy, poultry, and fish. You will learn how to make traditional dishes such as Moorish stews, Moroccan couscous, Syrian fattoush salad, and Tunisian harisa, as well as more modern creations. Moreover, Savoring Sephardic Cuisine offers helpful tips and techniques to streamline the preparation process, so readers can bring the flavors of the past to their kitchen table in no time.

The book also shines a light on the cooking customs and culinary history of Sephardic Jews, bringing to life the stories of famous family traditions and dishes that have been passed down from generation to generation. Savoring Sephardic Cuisine is an invitation to explore a unique corner of the world and discover the flavors and aromas of Sephardic cuisine. From the subtle and delicate to the exotic and bold, it will be a journey you won't soon forget.

Begin your journey into Sephardic flavors by mastering the basics. Learn the importance of using the right spices, and how to bring out the unique flavors of these ingredients with herbs, garlic, onion, and olive oil. Then, practice a few classic recipes so you can enjoy them any day of the week. Finally, let the book explore the more adventurous side of Sephardic cooking, as you bring the exotic flavors to your home and table. No matter which dishes you choose, you are sure to savor delicious meals and special memories that will last long after the last bite.

So, get ready to take a trip around the world with Savoring Sephardic Cuisine. With 101 delectable recipes, you will find yourself embracing the rich history and flavors of Sephardic cuisine.

1. Spinach Borekas

Spinach Borekas are a delicious pastry made by wrapping a creamy spinach filling in a buttery phyllo dough. This Middle Eastern dish is perfect for entertaining or can be enjoyed as a snack.

Serving: 8 servings
Preparation Time: 15 minutes
Ready Time: 45 minutes

Ingredients:
- 4 tablespoons of butter
- 1/2 teaspoon of salt
- 1/2 teaspoon of black pepper
- 1 small onion, finely chopped
- 10 ounces of frozen spinach, thawed and drained
- 8 ounces of feta cheese, crumbled
- 1/4 teaspoon of ground nutmeg
- 1/4 teaspoon of ground cinnamon
- 1 package of phyllo dough, thawed

Instructions:
1. Preheat oven to 350°F and melt 2 tablespoons of butter.
2. In a medium skillet, over medium heat, melt remaining 2 tablespoons of butter and add onion, salt, and pepper. Cook the onions until soft and golden.
3. Add spinach and cook until heated through. Remove skillet from heat and add feta cheese, nutmeg, and cinnamon. Stir to combine and set aside.
4. Grease a 9x13 inch baking pan and lay one sheet of phyllo dough across the bottom of the pan, brushing with melted butter. Repeat this process for another 7 to 10 layers of phyllo.
5. Spoon the spinach mixture onto the phyllo dough and spread evenly.
6. Layer the remaining phyllo sheet atop the spinach mixture, brushing each phyllo sheet with melted butter before adding the next sheet.
7. Bake for 30 minutes until golden brown. Cut into rectangular slices and serve.

Nutrition information: Serving size of 1 boreka has 200 calories, 12 g fat, 2 g saturated fat, 290 mg sodium, 16 g carbohydrates, 3 g fiber, and 6 g of protein.

2. Shakshuka

Shakshuka is a famous dish originally from the Middle East and North Africa which has become a breakfast favorite across the world. It's a simple yet delicious combination of eggs cooked in a flavorful tomato and pepper sauce.
Serving: 4
Preparation time: 15 minutes
Ready time: 30 minutes

Ingredients:
- 4 large eggs
- 2 tablespoons olive oil
- 1 red onion, finely chopped
- 2 cloves garlic, minced
- 1 red bell pepper, diced
- 2 cans (14.5 oz each) fire-roasted diced tomatoes
- 2 tablespoons tomato paste
- 1 teaspoon smoked paprika
- 1 teaspoon ground cumin
- ½ teaspoon salt
- ¼ teaspoon black pepper
- Chopped fresh parsley, for garnish

Instructions:
1. Preheat the oven to 375°F (190°C).
2. Heat the olive oil in a large skillet over medium heat. Add the onion and garlic and cook until soft and translucent, about 5 minutes.
3. Add the bell pepper and cook for an additional 4 minutes, stirring occasionally.
4. Add the canned tomatoes, tomato paste, paprika, cumin, salt, and pepper and stir until incorporated. Simmer until the sauce is thickened and bubbly, about 10 minutes.

5. Crack the eggs evenly around the pan and transfer the pan to the preheated oven.
6. Bake for 10 to 15 minutes, or until the eggs are just set and cooked through.
7. Garnish with parsley and serve.

Nutrition information: per serving (1/4 of the recipe):
Calories: 263
Protein: 11g
Fat: 17g
Carbohydrates: 16g
Fiber: 4g
Sugar: 8g
Sodium: 465mg

3. Matzo Ball Soup

Matzo ball soup is a comforting Jewish dish, made with fluffy matzo balls and chicken broth. It's perfect for a chilly evening or a Passover meal!
Serving: 4
Preparation Time: 15 minutes
Ready Time: 45 minutes

Ingredients:
- 2 tablespoons canola oil
- 2 carrots, diced
- 2 celery stalks, diced
- 1 medium onion, diced
- 1 clove garlic, minced
- 2 quarts chicken broth
- 2 tablespoons chopped fresh dill
  Salt and pepper, to taste
- 3 tablespoons matzo meal
- 2 eggs
- 2 tablespoons water

Instructions:

1. Heat the oil in a large pot over medium heat. Once the oil is hot, add in the carrots, celery, onion, and garlic and sauté until the vegetables are softened, about 7 minutes.
2. Pour in the chicken broth and bring to a simmer. Then add in the chopped dill, salt, and pepper.
3. In a medium bowl, mix together the matzo meal, eggs, and water until it forms a thick paste. With wet hands, shape the batter into 8 small balls.
4. Carefully add the matzo balls to the simmering broth and cook for 20 minutes.
5. Serve the soup with freshly grated black pepper.

Nutrition information:
Calories: 130, Fat: 6g, Sodium: 343mg, Carbohydrates: 12g, Protein: 5g

4. Moroccan Tagine

Moroccan Tagine is a traditional Moroccan dish prepared with slow cooking and includes the distinctively flavored Ingredients from Morocco. It has a deliciously savory flavor that will remind you of traditional Moroccan cuisine.
Serving: 4-5
Preparation time: 20 minutes
Ready time: 1 hour 10 minutes

Ingredients:
- 2 tablespoons olive oil
- 2 onions, diced
- 2 cloves garlic, minced
- 1 teaspoon ground ginger
- 2 teaspoons ground cumin
- 1 teaspoon ground coriander
- 1 teaspoon paprika
- 2 pounds chicken thighs, cut into large cubes
- 3 cups chicken broth
- 1 can (14.5 ounces) diced tomatoes
- 2/3 cup pitted dates, finely chopped
- 2 tablespoons fresh lemon juice
- 1/2 teaspoon saffron threads

- 1/2 teaspoon ground cinnamon
- 2 large potatoes, diced
- 1/2 cup green olives, pitted and halved
- 1/2 cup golden raisins
- 2 tablespoons chopped fresh cilantro

Instructions:
1. Heat the oil in a large Dutch oven over medium heat. Add the onions and garlic and cook for 5 minutes.
2. Add the ginger, cumin, coriander, and paprika and cook for another 2 minutes.
3. Add the chicken, broth, tomatoes, dates, lemon juice, saffron, and cinnamon, stirring to combine.
4. Bring the mixture to a boil, then reduce the heat to low, cover, and let simmer for 45 minutes.
5. Add the potatoes, olives, and raisins. Cover and cook for 20 minutes longer, or until the potatoes are tender.
6. Serve hot over cooked couscous, and garnish with fresh cilantro.

Nutrition information: (Per Serving)
Calories: 396, Total Fat: 8g, Saturated Fat: 2g, Cholesterol: 82mg, Sodium: 940mg, Carbohydrates: 52g, Fiber: 6g, Sugar: 26g, Protein: 28g

5. Sfenj (Moroccan Doughnuts)

Sfenj or Moroccan Doughnuts are a popular sweet pastry dish made with a dough made from fried dough, yeast, and plenty of sugar. They are served either plain or with a variety of toppings.
Serving: 6
Preparation time: 15 minutes
Ready time: 45 minutes

Ingredients:
• 2 packages active dry yeast
• 1/2 teaspoon sugar
• 1/2 cup warm water
• 5 1/2 cups flour
• 1 teaspoon salt

- 2 egg yolks
- 1/4 cup vegetable oil
- 2 quarts vegetable oil for frying
- 3/4 cup sugar for topping

Instructions:

1. Dissolve yeast and 1/2 teaspoon sugar in 1/2 cup warm water. Let sit for 10 minutes until foamy.
2. In a large bowl, combine the yeast mixture with the flour, salt, egg yolks, and vegetable oil. Knead dough until a soft and elastic texture is achieved. Divide the dough into 12 equal pieces and form into oblong shapes.
3. Heat 2 quarts of oil in a large pot or deep-fryer to 375°F. Carefully drop the doughnuts one at a time into the hot oil. Fry until golden brown and cooked through. Remove with a slotted spoon and drain on paper towels.
4. Immediately roll the doughnuts in the remaining sugar mixture. Serve the sfenj warm.

Nutrition information: Per serving: 238 Calories, 11g Fat (25% of calories from fat), 3g Protein, 32g Carbohydrate, 1g Dietary Fiber, 23mg Cholesterol, 219mg Sodium.

6. Ladino Sopa de Ajo

Ladino Sopa de Ajo is a hearty, flavorful soup that hails from the city of Toledo, Spain. This soup, made with garlic, potatoes, and other vegetables, is a hearty and satisfying soup that makes a great meal for any occasion.

Serving: 4
Preparation Time: 25 minutes
Ready Time: 55 minutes

Ingredients:

- 3 tablespoons olive oil
- 4 cloves garlic, minced
- 2 potatoes, diced
- 2 tomatoes, diced

- 6 cups vegetable broth
- 2 bay leaves
- 2 teaspoons paprika
- 2 teaspoons ground cumin
- Salt and pepper, to taste
- 2 tablespoons chopped fresh parsley

Instructions:
1. In a large stock pot, heat the olive oil over medium-high heat.
2. Add the garlic and sauté for 1 minute, stirring frequently.
3. Add the potatoes and tomatoes and sauté for 3 minutes.
4. Add the vegetable broth, bay leaves, paprika, and cumin.
5. Bring the mixture to a boil, reduce the heat to low, and simmer for 40 minutes.
6. Season with salt and pepper, to taste.
7. Finally, stir in the chopped parsley.
8. Serve warm.

Nutrition information:
Calories: 229
Fat: 9 g
Carbohydrates: 33 g
Protein: 4 g

7. Sabich

Sabich is a delicious Israeli dish consisting of pita stuffed with crispy fried eggplant, boiled eggs, tahini sauce and refreshing salads. It is a great option for lunch or as a light and nutritious dinner.
Serving: 4
Preparation Time: 30 Minutes
Ready Time: 45 Minutes

Ingredients:
- 2 whole pita bread
- 2 tablespoons olive oil
- 2 eggplants
- 2 tablespoons ground coriander

- 2 tablespoons ground cumin
- 2 boiled eggs
- 2 tablespoons chopped parsley
- 2 tablespoons tahini sauce
- 2 tomatoes
- ½ cucumber
- ½ onion
- 2 tablespoons lemon juice
- Salt and pepper

Instructions:
1. Preheat the oven to 350°F and brush the eggplant slices with olive oil.
2. Place the eggplant slices on a baking sheet lined with parchment paper.
3. Sprinkle the eggplant slices with coriander, cumin, salt and pepper.
4. Bake the eggplant in the oven for 20 minutes or until it is golden and crispy.
5. In the meantime, peel and slice the tomatoes and cucumber.
6. Finely chop the onion and parsley.
7. In a medium bowl, prepare the salad by combining the tomatoes, cucumber, onion, parsley, lemon juice, salt and pepper.
8. Transfer the salad to a serving plate.
9. Cut the eggs in half and place on the salad.
10. Heat the pita bread in the oven for 5 minutes or until golden and crispy.
11. To assemble the Sabich, spread tahini sauce on each pita half and place the baked eggplant slices on top.
12. Place a few salad leaves and sliced eggs on each on top of the eggplant.
13. Serve the Sabich with the prepared salad.

Nutrition information
Calories: 370, Fat: 15g, Carbs: 44g, Protein: 13g

8. Tabbouleh

Tabbouleh is a Middle Eastern salad dish usually made of tomatoes, parsley, bulgur, mint, onion, garlic, oil, and other herbs.
Serving: 4

Preparation Time: 10 minutes
Ready time: 10 minutes

Ingredients:
- 1 cup uncooked bulgur wheat
- 1/2 cup boiling water
- 2 cups finely chopped fresh parsley
- 1 cup diced tomatoes
- 2 tablespoons minced mint
- 1/2 cup diced onion
- 2 tablespoons olive oil
- 2 cloves minced garlic
- Juice of one lemon
- Salt and pepper to taste

Instructions:
1. Place bulgur wheat in a bowl and add boiling water. Set aside to cool.
2. In a separate bowl, mix together parsley, tomatoes, mint, onion and garlic.
3. Once the bulgur wheat has cooled, add it to the other Ingredients and mix together.
4. Drizzle olive oil and lemon juice over the mixture and season with salt and pepper.

Nutrition information:
1 Serving has approximately 160 calories, 6.5g fat, 20g carbohydrates, and 4g protein.

9. Sephardic Spinach Patties

Sephardic Spinach Patties are one of the most popular Sephardic dishes that can be served as a side dish or a main meal. This recipe is incredibly easy to make and comes together in about 10 minutes.
Serving: 4
Preparation Time: 10 mins
Ready Time: 30 minutes

Ingredients:

- 2 cups frozen spinach
- 1 onion, diced
- 2 cloves garlic, minced
- 2 eggs
- 1 teaspoon salt
- ½ teaspoon ground black pepper
- 2 teaspoons baking powder
- ½ cup all-purpose flour
- ¾ cup breadcrumbs
- Oil, for frying

Instructions:
1. Preheat oven to 400°F (200°C).
2. Place frozen spinach, onion, and garlic in a food processor and process until well chopped.
3. In a large bowl, whisk together eggs, salt, pepper, baking powder, and flour until well combined.
4. Add the chopped spinach mixture and stir to combine.
5. Form the mixture into 4-inch (10 cm) patties and coat each patty with breadcrumbs on both sides.
6. Heat oil in a skillet over medium-high heat and fry the patties for 3-4 minutes on each side until golden brown and crispy.
7. Place the patties on a baking sheet and bake in the preheated oven for 15 minutes.

Nutrition information:
Calories: 214, Fat: 10g, Carbohydrates: 18g, Protein: 12g, Cholesterol: 81mg, Sodium: 708mg, Fiber: 2g, Sugar: 2g.

10. Chicken Marbella

Chicken Marbella is an elegant dish with origins in Jewish Northern African cooking. It is a tangy combination of Ingredients and a great way to dress up an ordinary chicken dinner.
Serving:
Serves 4
Preparation Time:
15 minutes

Ready Time:
2 hours

Ingredients:
- 4 pounds of chicken pieces (legs, thighs and wings work best)
- 1/2 cup olive oil
- 1/2 cup red wine vinegar
- 1/3 cup dried oregano
- 6 cloves of garlic, minced
- 1 teaspoon salt
- 1 tablespoon sugar
- 1 teaspoon black pepper
- 1/2 cup prunes, halved and pitted
- 1/2 cup green olives, pitted
- 1/2 cup capers
- 3 bay leaves
- 2 oranges, juice and zest

Instructions:
1. Preheat oven to 350°F (176°C).
2. In a large bowl, combine olive oil, red wine vinegar, oregano, garlic, salt, sugar, and black pepper. Add chicken pieces and coat in the marinade.
3. Place chicken in a 9x13 inch baking dish. Add prunes, olives, capers, bay leaves, orange zest and orange juice.
4. Bake in the preheated oven for 1 1/2 to 2 hours, or until chicken is cooked through and juices run clear.

Nutrition information:
Serving size: 1 piece
Calories: 328 kcal, Fat: 13.4g, Carbohydrates: 9.9g, Fiber: 2.4g, Protein: 31.8g

11. Keftes de Espinaca (Spinach Meatballs)

This recipe for Keftes de Espinaca (Spinach Meatballs) offers a delicious vegetarian alternative to traditional meatballs. They are packed full of flavorful Ingredients and are sure to please any crowd.

Serving: 4-6
Preparation Time: 10 minutes
Ready Time: 40 minutes

Ingredients:
- 2 cloves of garlic, minced
- 2 tablespoons of olive oil
- 3/4 pound of fresh spinach
- 1/4 cup of plain breadcrumbs
- 3 tablespoons of freshly chopped parsley
- 2 large eggs
- 2 tablespoons of grated Parmesan cheese
- 1/2 teaspoon of ground nutmeg
- Salt and pepper to taste
- Vegetable oil for frying

Instructions:
1. In a large skillet over medium heat, add the olive oil. When the oil is hot, add the minced garlic and saute for 1-2 minutes until fragrant.
2. Add the spinach and saute for 3-4 minutes until wilted. Remove from the heat and add to a large bowl.
3. Add the breadcrumbs, parsley, eggs, Parmesan cheese, nutmeg, salt, and pepper to the spinach. Mix with a spoon until everything is combined.
4. Using your hands, form the mixture into small balls, about 1-2 inches in diameter.
5. In a large skillet, heat the vegetable oil over medium heat. When the oil is hot, add the meatballs to the skillet and cook for about 5 minutes, flipping them every few minutes until they are golden brown and cooked through.
6. Serve with your favorite dipping sauce and enjoy!

Nutrition information: 1 Serving (4-6): Approximately 150 calories, 11.7g fat, 5.3g carbohydrates, 7.7g protein

12. Flan

Flan is a popular custard dessert from Spanish and Latin American cuisines. It is typically made with eggs, cream or milk, and sugar for a smooth, creamy, and sweet finish.
Serving: Serves 8-10
Preparation time: 25 minutes
Ready time: 1 hour 15 minutes

Ingredients:
4 eggs
2 cups cream
1/2 cup sweetened condensed milk
3/4 cup white sugar
1 teaspoon vanilla extract
1/4 teaspoon salt

Instructions:
1. Preheat oven to 350°F (175°C). Grease an 8-inch or 9-inch round pan and line with parchment paper.
2. In a large bowl, whisk together eggs, cream, sweetened condensed milk, sugar, vanilla, and salt until completely combined.
3. Pour mixture through a strainer into the prepared pan. Bake in preheated oven for 45 minutes, or until slightly golden on top.
4. Cool flan at room temperature for 15 minutes before transferring to refrigerator to refrigerate for at least 1 hour.
5. Serve chilled as desired.

Nutrition information: Per serving: Calories 200, Total Fat 9 g (Saturated Fat 5.2 g, Trans Fat 0 g), Cholesterol 79 mg, Sodium 70 mg, Total Carbohydrate 24 g (Dietary Fiber 0 g, Total Sugars 19 g, Added Sugars 11 g), Protein 6 g.

13. Tzatziki

Tzatziki is a delicious Greek yogurt-based sauce, made with sour cream, garlic, cucumbers, and fresh herbs like dill and mint. It's a wonderful sauce for grilled meats, vegetables, or as a dip for pita chips.
Serving: 4-6
Preparation Time: 10 minutes

Ready Time: 30 minutes

Ingredients:
-1 cup plain Greek yogurt
-1/2 cucumber, peeled, seeded, and diced
-2 cloves garlic, minced
-1/4 cup sour cream
-2 teaspoons fresh dill
-1 teaspoon fresh mint
-1 tablespoon freshly squeezed lemon juice
-Salt and pepper to taste

Instructions:
1. In a large bowl, combine Greek yogurt, cucumber, garlic, sour cream, dill, mint, lemon juice, and salt and pepper to taste.
2. Mix thoroughly and refrigerate for at least 30 minutes.
3. Serve with grilled chicken, vegetables, or as a dip for pita chips.

Nutrition information:
1 serving (1/6 of recipe) contains:
Calories: 82, Fat: 6 g, Saturated fat: 3 g, Carbohydrates: 5 g, Protein: 4 g, Cholesterol: 13 mg, Sodium: 143 mg.

14. Lutenitsa

Lutenitsa is a delicious dish from Bulgaria. It is a type of very thick relish or paste made from roasted peppers, tomatoes, and eggplants. It is often served as a side dish.
Serving: 8 Servings
Preparation Time: 10 minutes
Ready Time: 25 minutes

Ingredients:
• 6 red bell peppers
• 2 eggplants
• 5 large tomatoes
• 3 cloves of garlic
• 2 tablespoons of tomato paste

- ½ teaspoon of ground black pepper
- salt to taste
- ¼ cup of olive oil

Instructions:
1. Preheat oven to 400 degrees.
2. Cut the bell peppers, eggplants, and tomatoes into slices. Spread them on a baking tray lined with parchment paper.
3. Roast the vegetables for 20 minutes or until they are tender.
4. While the vegetables are roasting, mince the garlic.
5. When the vegetables are done, place them in a pot with the tomato paste, garlic, ground black pepper, salt, and olive oil.
6. Mash the vegetables until they form a thick paste.
7. Allow the lutenitsa to cool before serving.

Nutrition information: Serving size: 2 tablespoons; Calories: 70; Fat: 5g; Sodium: 15mg; Carbohydrates: 5g; Protein: 1g.

15. Eggplant Moussaka

Eggplant Moussaka is a classic Greek dish with a rich, hearty sauce and creamy layers of eggplant and cheese goodness.
Serving: 4-6 people
Preparation Time: 30 minutes
Ready Time: 1 hour and 15 minutes

Ingredients:
- 2 large eggplants, sliced
- 2 tablespoons olive oil
- 1 onion, chopped
- 1 garlic clove, minced
- 2 tablespoons tomato paste
- 2 tablespoons all purpose flour
- 2 cups chicken or vegetable broth
- 1 teaspoon dried oregano
- 2 tablespoons butter
- 2 eggs
- 2 tablespoons grated Parmesan cheese

- 2 cups ricotta cheese
- Salt and freshly ground black pepper

Instructions:
1. Preheat oven to 375 degrees F.
2. Grease a 9x13-inch baking dish.
3. Arrange the eggplant slices in the bottom of the dish.
4. Heat 1 tablespoon olive oil in a skillet over medium heat and sauté the onion and garlic for 5 minutes.
5. Add tomato paste, flour, chicken broth, oregano and remaining oil. Simmer until thickened.
6. Pour the mixture over the eggplant slices.
7. In the same skillet, melt the butter and whisk in the eggs until smooth.
8. Add the Parmesan and ricotta cheese and season with salt and pepper.
9. Spread the cheese mixture over the eggplant and sauce.
10. Bake for 40 minutes until golden brown.

Nutrition information: (Per Serving): 288 Calories; 16g Fat; 16g Protein; 20g Carbohydrate; 3.9g Fiber; 572mg Sodium

16. Fava Bean Dip

This delicious Fava Bean Dip is a creamy and flavorful appetizer perfect for any occasion! It is made with fava beans, fresh herbs, and seasonings.
Serving: Makes 8-10 servings
Preparation Time: 10 minutes
Ready Time: 30 minutes

Ingredients:
- 2 cups cooked fava beans
- 2 cloves garlic, minced
- 1 teaspoon onion powder
- 3 tablespoons fresh parsley, chopped
- 2 tablespoons lemon juice
- 2 teaspoons olive oil
- Salt and pepper to taste

Instructions:

1. Place the fava beans, garlic, onion powder, parsley, lemon juice and olive oil into a food processor.
2. Pulse the mixture until it is smooth and creamy.
3. Season with salt and pepper to taste.
4. Transfer the dip to a bowl and garnish with fresh herbs.
5. Serve with slices of rustic French bread or crackers.

Nutrition information: Each serving of Fava Bean Dip (2 tablespoons) contains approximately 90 calories, 2.5g fat, 10g carbohydrates, 5g protein and 2g fiber.

17. Sfouf (Semolina Cake)

Sfouf is a traditional Lebanese semolina cake that is popular throughout the Middle Eastern and Mediterranean region. It is lightly sweetened and laced with orange blossom and mahlab aromas. It is a delightful balance of the sunny flavours of citrus and rosewater, baked to perfection.
Serving: 16
Preparation Time: 30 minutes
Ready Time: 45 minutes

Ingredients:
- 2 cups fine semolina
- 1 cup granulated sugar
- 1 cup clarified butter (ghee)
- 1/2 cup whole milk
- 2 large eggs
- 2 tablespoons orange blossom water
- 2 teaspoons ground mahlab
- 1 teaspoon baking powder
- 2 tablespoons pine nuts, toasted
- 2 tablespoons orange zest
- 2 tablespoons chopped pistachios

Instructions:
1. Preheat the oven to 350°F (180°C). Grease an 8-inch (20 cm) round or square baking pan with butter or pan spray.

2. In a large bowl, mix together the semolina, sugar, clarified butter, milk, eggs, orange blossom water, mahlab, and baking powder until all the Ingredients are evenly combined.

3. Pour the semolina batter into the prepared pan. Top with the toasted pine nuts, orange zest, and chopped pistachios.

4. Bake for 30 minutes or until the top is golden brown.

5. Allow the cake to cool completely before cutting and serving.

Nutrition information:
Calories: 300; Fat: 15g; Saturated fat: 9g; Carbohydrates: 33g; Sugar: 17g; Protein: 4g; Sodium: 130mg; Cholesterol: 80mg.

18. Sephardic Brisket

Sephardic Brisket is a classic kosher staple in the Jewish kitchen. It is a slow-cooked braised brisket that is easy to make, requiring only a few basic Ingredients.

Serving: 6 people
Preparation time: 10 minutes
Ready time: 3 hours

Ingredients:
- 3 lbs brisket
- 1 large onion, diced
- 2 cloves garlic, minced
- 1/4 cup dry white wine or apple juice
- 1/4 cup tomato paste
- 1/4 cup honey
- 1/2 tsp ground allspice
- 1/2 tsp ground cinnamon

Instructions:
1. Preheat oven to 350°F.
2. Place the brisket in a large roasting pan and season with salt and pepper.
3. In a medium bowl, combine the onion, garlic, white wine, tomato paste, honey and spices.
4. Pour the mixture over the brisket and spread evenly.

5. Cover the pan with aluminum foil and bake for 2 to 3 hours, or until the brisket is tender.
6. Remove from the oven and let cool before serving.

Nutrition information: Calories 571; Total Fat 24.6g; Total Carbohydrate 13.6g; Dietary Fiber 2.3g; Protein 63.4g

19. Bosnian Burek

Bosnian burek is an iconic dish in Bosnia and Herzegovina. It is an unleavened pastry made with thin layers of flaky dough filled with either ground beef, sheep cheese, spinach or potatoes.
Serving: 4-6
Preparation time: 25 minutes
Ready time: 1 hour

Ingredients:
• 2 tablespoons olive oil
• 1 large onion, diced
• 500g ground beef
• Salt
• 300g feta cheese, crumbled
• 2 eggs, beaten
• 4 sheets filo pastry

Instructions:
1. Preheat oven to 375°F (190°C).
2. Heat a large frying pan over medium heat and add olive oil.
3. Add the onions and cook for 2 minutes.
4. Add the ground beef and cook until the beef is no longer pink.
5. Add salt to taste and remove from heat.
6. Mix in the feta cheese.
7. In a medium bowl, beat the eggs and add to the beef and cheese mixture.
8. Line a greased baking pan with 4 sheets of filo pastry.
9. Spread the beef and cheese mixture over the pastry.
10. Cover with the remaining sheets of filo pastry.
11. Use a pastry brush to brush with beaten egg.

12. Bake in preheated oven for 45 minutes.

Nutrition information: Per serving: Calories: 354 Fat: 23.5g Protein: 22.1g Carbohydrate: 13.7g Sodium: 731mg

20. Migas

Migas is a traditional Spanish dish made of eggs and fried tortilla or breadcrumbs. It is a flavorful, colorful, and filling dish that makes for a delicious breakfast or brunch option.
Serving: 4
Preparation Time: 15 minutes
Ready Time: 25 minutes

Ingredients:
- 4 tablespoons olive oil
- 4 slices stale or day-old bread, torn into small pieces
- 2 cloves of garlic, minced
- 1 teaspoon smoked paprika
- 1/2 yellow onion, diced
- 1/2 green bell pepper, diced
- 1/2 red bell pepper, diced
- 2 tomatoes, chopped
- 6 large eggs
- 2 tablespoons flat-leaf parsley, finely chopped
- Salt, to taste
- Freshly ground black pepper, to taste

Instructions:
1. Heat olive oil in a large frying pan over medium heat.
2. Add the bread to the pan and fry until golden brown, about 5 minutes.
3. Add the garlic, paprika, onions, bell peppers and tomatoes to the pan and cook until the vegetables are soft, about 5 minutes.
4. In a medium bowl, whisk together the eggs with parsley, salt, and pepper.
5. Add the eggs to the pan and gently combine with the other Ingredients.

6. Cook until the egg mixture is set, about 10 minutes.

Nutrition information:
Calories: 302, Carbohydrates: 21g, Fat: 19g, Protein: 12g, Cholesterol: 174mg, Sodium: 441mg, Potassium: 422mg, Fiber: 3g, Sugar: 3g.

21. Turkish Delight

Turkish Delight is a delightful treat made from sugar and starch and flavored with rosewater, lemon or mint. Unlike other desserts, Turkish Delight is more like a jelly or chewy candy.
Serving: Makes 24 pieces
Preparation time: 10 minutes
Ready time: 45 minutes

Ingredients:
- 2 cups granulated sugar
- 2/3 cups cold water
- 3 tablespoons cornstarch
- 3/4 cup corn syrup
- 2 tablespoons lemon juice
- 2 teaspoons rosewater
- 1 teaspoon orange blossom water
- 2 tablespoons butter
- 1/2 teaspoon cream of tartar
- Powdered sugar, for dusting
- Food coloring, optional

Instructions:
1. In a medium saucepan over low heat, combine the sugar, cold water and cornstarch. Cook, stirring carefully, until the mixture takes on a custard-like consistency.
2. Add the corn syrup, lemon juice, rosewater, orange blossom water and butter, stirring to combine. Add the cream of tartar.
3. Increase the heat to medium and cook, stirring often, for about 25 minutes. The mixture should thicken and take on an almost frothy texture.
4. Add in food coloring, if desired.

5. Pour the mixture into a lightly greased 8x8 inch baking dish. Let cool for about 10 minutes before cutting into cubes.
6. Dust with powdered sugar and enjoy.

Nutrition information:
Each piece contains 188 calories, 0 g fat, 42 g carbohydrates, and 12 g sugar.

22. Imjadara (Lentil and Rice Pilaf)

Imjadara is a flavorful and nutritious traditional Levantine lentil and rice pilaf dish that is packed with warm Middle Eastern spices. It is served as a side dish but can also be served as a vegetarian main.
Serving: 4
Preparation time: 15 minutes
Ready time: 30 minutes

Ingredients:
• 2 tablespoons olive oil
• 1 medium yellow onion, diced
• 1 1/2 teaspoons ground cumin
• 1/2 teaspoon cinnamon
• 1/2 teaspoon smoked paprika
• 1/2 teaspoon turmeric
• 1 teaspoon ground coriander
• 1 cup long grain rice, rinsed puls 1-2 times
• 2 1/4 cup vegetable broth
• 1/2 cup French green lentils, rinsed
• 1/4 cup chopped parsley
• 2 tablespoons freshly squeezed lemon juice
• 1 teaspoon salt
• Freshly ground pepper

Instructions:
1. Heat the oil in a medium pot over medium heat. Add the onion, cumin, cinnamon, smoked paprika, turmeric, and coriander to the pot and stir. Cook until the onions become soft and golden, for about 5 minutes.

2. Add the rice and stir for 1-2 minutes, until lightly toasted. Add the vegetable broth, lentils, parsley, lemon juice, salt and pepper to the pot, and stir again.

3. Cover the pot with a lid, and reduce the heat to low. Cook the imjadara for about 15-20 minutes, until all the liquid has been absorbed and the rice and lentils are cooked through.

4. Taste it and adjust seasonings if needed. Serve warm.

Nutrition information: Per serving, Imjadara contains 302 calories, 8 g fat, 44 g carbohydrate, and 10 g protein.

23. Burekas

Burekas is a flaky pastry filled with cheese and spices that is popular throughout the Middle East and North Africa. It's a favorite for breakfast or just a snack and easy to make with prepared puff pastry.
Serving: 10 burekas
Preparation Time: 15 minutes
Ready Time: 40 minutes

Ingredients:
• 2 sheets frozen puff pastry
• 500 grams of feta cheese
• 100 grams of grated cheese
• 3 eggs
• 1 large onion, minced
• 2 tablespoons parsley, minced
• 2 tablespoons olive oil

Instructions:
1. Preheat the oven to 200 °C/ 400 °F.
2. Defrost the pastry and lay them both out on a lightly floured surface.
3. In a bowl, beat the eggs and add the feta, grated cheese, minced onion, parsley, and olive oil. Mix until blended.
4. Cut the pastry into 10 pieces. Place a spoonful of filling in the centre of each piece of pastry.
5. Fold one side of the pastry over the filling and press around the edges to seal.

6. Place the pastries on a greased baking sheet.
7. Bake for 20-25 minutes, or until the burekas turn a light golden colour.

Nutrition information:
Calories: 130 | Protein: 6g | Fat: 8g | Carbs: 8g | Sodium: 215mg

24. Kofta Kebabs

Kofta Kebabs are an incredibly delicious Middle Eastern dish featuring flavorful meatballs grilled to perfection. Not only is it a fun and nutritious meal for the whole family to enjoy, but it is also incredibly easy to prepare.
Serving: 6-8
Preparation time: 20 minutes
Ready time: 20-30 minutes

Ingredients:
-1 pound ground beef
-2 teaspoons garlic paste
-1 teaspoon cumin powder
-1 teaspoon coriander powder
-1/2 teaspoon turmeric powder
-1 medium onion, finely chopped
-2 tablespoons freshly chopped parsley
-1 teaspoon salt
-1/4 teaspoon pepper
-2 tablespoons olive oil

Instructions:
1. In a bowl, combine ground beef, garlic paste, cumin powder, coriander powder, turmeric powder, onion, parsley, salt, and pepper. Mix until combined.
2. Form the mixture into 12 equal-sized kebabs.
3. Heat olive oil in a large skillet over medium-high heat.
4. Add kebabs and cook for 10-15 minutes, turning them occasionally, until golden brown and cooked through.
5. Serve immediately.

Nutrition information:
Serving size: 1 kebab
Calories: 187
Total Fat: 10.5g
Cholesterol: 41mg
Sodium: 308mg
Total Carbohydrates: 5.6g
Protein: 17.5g

25. Cholent

Cholent is a traditional Jewish stew that is cooked for a long period of time at low heat. It's rich in flavor and is enjoyed by people of all backgrounds.
Serving: 8
Preparation Time: 10 minutes
Ready Time: 8-12 hours

Ingredients:
2 pounds beef chuck or stew meat
2 medium onions, diced
2 cloves garlic, minced
2 tablespoons vegetable oil
1 tablespoon paprika
2 teaspoons ground cumin
2 large potatoes, peeled and diced
3 carrots, chopped
1 cup dried lima beans
1 cup barley
3 tablespoons ketchup
6 cups low-sodium beef broth
Salt and freshly ground black pepper, to taste

Instructions:
1. Preheat the oven to 250°F.
2. Heat the oil in a large oven-safe pot over medium heat. Cook the onion and garlic until fragrant.

3. Add the beef and cook until browned. Add the paprika and cumin. Cook for 1 minute.
4. Add the potatoes, carrots, lima beans, barley, ketchup, beef broth, and salt and pepper. Bring to a gentle simmer.
5. Place the lid on the pot and transfer it to the oven. Cook for 8 to 12 hours.
6. Serve the cholent warm.

Nutrition information: Calories: 288, Fat: 11.4g, Carbs: 28.7g, Protein: 17.6g, Fiber: 4.5g, Sodium: 413mg

26. Fattoush Salad

Fattoush is a Middle Eastern salad made with a combination of vegetables, herbs, and crunchy pita chips. It is dressed in a lemony, olive oil and spices. It can be served as a side, as a main dish, or as part of a mezze platter.
Serving: 4
Preparation Time: 10 minutes
Ready Time: 10 minutes

Ingredients:
2 medium tomatoes, diced
1/2 cucumber, diced
1/2 bell pepper, diced
1/2 small onion, diced
1/4 cup fresh parsley, chopped
1/4 cup fresh mint leaves, chopped
1/4 cup fresh lemon juice
2 tablespoons extra-virgin olive oil
1/2 teaspoon ground sumac
1/2 teaspoon sea salt
1/4 teaspoon ground black pepper
2 cups pita chips, roughly chopped

Instructions:
1. In a large bowl, combine diced tomatoes, cucumber, bell pepper, onion, parsley, and mint leaves.

2. In a small bowl, whisk together lemon juice, olive oil, sumac, salt, and pepper. Drizzle the dressing over the salad and toss to combine.
3. Just before serving, sprinkle with the pita chips and toss again.

Nutrition information:
Calories: 184
Fat: 9g
Carbohydrates: 24g
Fiber: 3g
Protein: 4g

27. Kibbeh

Kibbeh is a tasty Middle Eastern dish usually made from minced lamb, bulgur, and spices. It can be served raw, cooked as a pastry, or even fried. It's a perfect dish for entertaining or to have as a main course.
Serving: 6
Preparation Time: 30 minutes
Ready Time: 3 hours

Ingredients:
• 2 cups fine bulgur
• 2 lbs ground lamb
• 1 onion, finely chopped
• 1/4 cup minced fresh parsley
• 1/4 cup olive oil
• 1 teaspoon ground allspice
• 1 teaspoon ground cinnamon
• 1 teaspoon freshly ground black pepper
• 2 teaspoons sea salt

Instructions:
1. Soak the bulgur in water for 30 minutes.
2. In a large bowl, combine the ground lamb, onion, parsley, olive oil, allspice, cinnamon, black pepper, and sea salt.
3. Using your hands, mix the Ingredients until they are well combined.
4. Drain the bulgur, then add it to the meat mixture.
5. Knead the mixture with your hands until it forms a dough.

6. Form the meat mixture into balls or logs, and then flatten them into patties or discs.
7. Heat a skillet over medium-high heat, and then cook the kibbeh for 2-3 minutes on each side until golden brown.

Nutrition information: (per serving)
• Calories: 430
• Fat: 20g
• Carbs: 30g
• Protein: 25g

28. Bastilla

Bastilla is an exotic Moroccan dish made of baked pigeon or chicken, layers of warka pastry, and warm spices. It is usually served as a starter or main dish, and can be served hot or cold.
Serving: 4 servings
Preparation time: 30 minutes
Ready Time: 1 hour

Ingredients:
- 500g skinless chicken, cubed
- 1 onion, finely chopped
- 2 garlic cloves, finely chopped
- 1 teaspoon ground ginger
- 1 teaspoon ground cinnamon
- 2 tablespoon olive oil
- 4 tablespoons butter
- 6-8 sheets warka pastry
- 2 tablespoons chopped almonds
- 2 tablespoons chopped pistachios
- 4-5 tablespoons icing sugar

Instructions:
1. Preheat oven to 200°C.
2. Heat the olive oil in a frying pan over medium heat. Add the cubed chicken, onion and garlic and fry until chicken is cooked through.

3. Add in the ground ginger and cinnamon and fry for another few minutes.
4. Grease a baking tray with 2 tablespoons of butter. Place the warka pastry sheets on the baking tray and spread spoonfuls of the chicken mixture on each sheet.
5. Top with the remaining butter, almonds, and pistachios. Sprinkle the icing sugar on top.
6. Fold over the edges of each sheet to enclose the filling.
7. Bake in the oven for 30 minutes, or until the warka pastry is golden and crispy.
8. Serve warm or cold.

Nutrition information
Calories: 487
Fat: 29.8g
Carbohydrates: 32.9g
Protein: 24.1g

29. Kufta

This classic Persian dish, known as Kufta, is an amazingly flavorful and tender lamb meatball, simmered in a tart and zesty tomato sauce. This version of Kufta is sure to be a crowd favorite!
Serving: 4-6
Preparation time: 10 minutes
Ready time: 40 minutes

Ingredients:
•1 lb ground lamb
•1 cup finely chopped onion
•2 large eggs
•3 cloves garlic, minced
•2 tablespoons freshly chopped parsley
•1 teaspoon ground cinnamon
•1 teaspoon ground cumin
•1 teaspoon ground coriander
•1 teaspoon freshly ground black pepper
•2 tablespoons olive oil

•2 cups tomato sauce
•Salt to taste

Instructions:
1. In a large bowl, combine the ground lamb, onion, eggs, garlic, parsley, cinnamon, cumin, coriander, black pepper, and salt. Mix well to combine.
2. Using your hands, form the meat mixture into 18-24 equal-sized balls.
3. Heat the olive oil in a large skillet over medium heat. Add the kufta balls and cook until lightly browned, about 10 minutes.
4. Add the tomato sauce to the pan and bring to a simmer. Reduce the heat to low and cover. Simmer for 30 minutes.
5. Serve hot.

Nutrition information:
Calories: 356; Total Fat: 24g; Saturated Fat: 8g; Cholesterol: 130mg; Sodium: 185mg; Carbohydrates: 7g; Fiber: 1g; Protein: 28g

30. Eggplant Salad

This easy vegan Eggplant Salad is a flavorful and light side dish. It's made with simple Ingredients and doesn't take too much time to throw together!
Serving: 4
Preparation time: 10 minutes
Ready time: 35 minutes

Ingredients:
• 2 medium eggplants, cut into 1 inch cubes
• 2 tablespoons olive oil
• ¼ cup fresh parsley, chopped
• 2 tablespoons balsamic vinegar
• 1 garlic clove, pressed or minced
• Salt and pepper to taste

Instructions:
1. Preheat oven to 400°F and line a baking sheet with parchment paper.

2. Arrange eggplant cubes in a single layer on the baking sheet. Drizzle with olive oil and season with salt and pepper.
3. Roast in preheated oven for 25-30 minutes, until eggplant is golden and tender.
4. In a mixing bowl, combine eggplant cubes, parsley, balsamic vinegar and garlic. Stir until everything is well combined.
5. Serve immediately or chill in refrigerator for 1-2 hours.

Nutrition information: per serving: 117 calories; 8.5 g fat; 9.8 g carbohydrates; 1.6 g protein; 2.5 g fiber

31. Moroccan Lamb Stew

Moroccan Lamb Stew is a comforting and warming meal that is naturally gluten-free and full of rich flavor. Sautéed vegetables, tender lamb, fragrant spices, and a hint of sweetness from the sweet potatoes are all combined in a one-pot meal that pairs perfectly with a crusty piece of bread.
Serving: 8-10
Preparation Time: 15 minutes
Ready Time: 4 hours

Ingredients:
- 2 pounds lamb shoulder, cut into 1-in cubes
- 4 cloves garlic, minced
- 2 tablespoons olive oil
- 1 onion, chopped
- 1 red bell pepper, seeded and chopped
- 1 teaspoon ground ginger
- 2 teaspoons ground cumin
- 2 teaspoons paprika
- 2 teaspoons turmeric
- 1 teaspoon ground cinnamon
- 1 teaspoon ground coriander
- 2 teaspoons salt
- 1 teaspoon black pepper
- 2 cups chicken broth
- 2 large sweet potatoes, peeled and cubed

- 1/4 cup golden raisins
- 1/4 cup chopped fresh cilantro

Instructions:
1. In a large pot on medium-high heat, heat the olive oil.
2. Add the lamb cubes, season them with the salt and pepper and sautéuntil golden brown.
3. Add the garlic, onion, and bell pepper and sauté until soft.
4. Add the ginger, cumin, paprika, turmeric, cinnamon, and coriander and stir to combine.
5. Add the chicken broth, sweet potatoes, and raisins and bring to a boil.
6. Reduce the heat to low and simmer, uncovered, for 3-4 hours, stirring occasionally, until the lamb is tender.
7. Stir in the cilantro and adjust for seasoning. Serve with crusty bread.

Nutrition information:
Calories: 570 kcal, Fat: 25 g, Saturated Fat: 8 g, Cholesterol: 130 mg, Sodium: 880 mg, Potassium: 1120 mg, Carbohydrates: 38 g, Fiber: 7 g, Sugar: 9 g, Protein: 43 g, Vitamin A: 350%, Vitamin C: 30%, Calcium: 40%, Iron: 8%

32. Bourekas with Cheese and Spinach

Bourekas with Cheese and Spinach is a flavorful fried pastry filled with a creamy combination of cheese and spinach. This comforting dish is great for appetizers or side dishes, as well as a delicious snack.
Serving: 8 pieces
Preparation time: 15 minutes
Ready time: 30 minutes

Ingredients:
-1 sheet of pastry dough, thawed and rolled into a rectangle
-1 cup of crumbled cheese
-1 cup of cooked, chopped spinach
-1/4 cup of olive oil
-Salt and pepper, to taste

Instructions:

1. Preheat oven to 375 degrees F.
2. Place the pastry sheet onto a baking sheet.
3. In a bowl, combine the cheese, spinach, olive oil, and seasonings. Mix to combine.
4. Spread the cheese and spinach mixture on the pastry sheet, leaving a ½ inch border on the edges.
5. Fold the edges of the pastry sheet inwards, forming a rectangle.
6. Bake for 15 to 20 minutes until the pastry is golden and crisp.
7. Cut into 8 even squares and serve warm.

Nutrition information:
Calories: 176, Fat: 9g, Cholesterol: 10mg, Sodium: 119mg, Carbohydrates: 16g, Protein: 5g

33. Samosa

Samosas are a popular Indian snack that is packed full of flavors. Traditionally made from a flaky pastry, it is filled with spiced potatoes, peas and onions and then fried until golden and crispy. Servings: 4 Preparation Time: 30 minutes Ready Time: 45 minutes

Ingredients:
- 2 teaspoons of oil
- 1 small onion, chopped
- 2 cloves of garlic, minced
- 1 teaspoon of grated ginger
- 1 teaspoon of ground cumin
- 1 teaspoon of garam masala
- ½ teaspoon of turmeric
- ½ teaspoon of ground coriander
- ½ teaspoon of cayenne pepper
- 2 large potatoes, peeled and diced
  1 cup of peas
- ¼ cup of cilantro, chopped
- Salt and pepper, to taste
- 2 packages store-bought pastry or homemade
- 2-3 cups of oil, for frying

Instructions:

1. Heat the oil in a large skillet over medium heat. Add the onion and cook until lightly browned, about 5 minutes.
2. Add the garlic, ginger, cumin, garam masala, turmeric, coriander, and cayenne pepper and cook for 1 minute.
3. Add the potatoes and toss to coat with the spices. Cook for 5 minutes.
4. Add the peas and cilantro and cook until the potatoes are tender, about 10 minutes.
5. Remove from the heat and season with salt and pepper. Let cool slightly.
6. Cut the pastry into four-inch circles. Place about two tablespoons of the filling in the center of each circle. Then fold the pastry over the filling and seal the edges with a fork.
7. Heat the oil in a medium-sized pot over medium heat. Add the samosas and fry until golden and crisp, about 5 minutes.
8. Drain on paper towels and serve warm. Nutrition information:
Calories per serving: 83
Fat: 3.4g
Carbohydrates: 9.7g
Protein: 2.4g

34. Moussaka

Moussaka is an eggplant-based traditional Greek dish. It consists of layers of eggplant slices baked in a delicious spiced beef tomato sauce and is typically finished with a creamy béchamel sauce.
Serving: 4
Preparation Time: 20 minutes
Ready Time: 55 minutes

Ingredients:
- 2 large eggplants, peeled and sliced
- 1 tablespoon of olive oil
- 1 onion, chopped
- 2 cloves garlic, crushed
- 500 g ground beef
- 400 g tinned tomatoes
- 2 tablespoons of tomato paste

- 2 tablespoons of red wine or brandy
- 2 teaspoons of ground paprika
- 1 teaspoon of ground cinnamon
- 2 tablespoons of chopped parsley
- Salt and freshly ground pepper, to taste

Instructions:

1. Preheat oven to 180°C. Place the eggplant on a baking tray and brush with olive oil. Bake in preheated oven for 15 minutes, or until golden brown.
2. Meanwhile, heat the remaining olive oil in a large saucepan over medium heat. Add the onion and garlic and cook for 10 minutes, or until softened.
3. Add the ground beef and cook until browned. Stir in the tomato puree, tinned tomatoes, red wine (or brandy), paprika, cinnamon, parsley, salt and pepper and simmer for 10 minutes.
4. Remove the eggplant from the oven and layer the eggplant in the bottom of an oven proof baking dish. Top with the beef tomato sauce.
5. Make a béchamel sauce (recipe here) and spread it over the top of the moussaka.
6. Bake in preheated oven for 30 minutes, or until golden brown.

Nutrition information:

- Calories: 367
- Protein: 16 g
- Fat: 14 g
- Carbohydrates: 34 g
- Sodium: 313 mg

35. Sambusak

Sambusak is a popular snack in the Middle East that is usually served as an appetizer or as a snack. It is made with a pastry dough filled with spiced mix of ground beef or cheese.
Serving: 6
Preparation Time: 45 minutes
Ready Time: 1 hour

Ingredients:
1 package Puff Pastry
1 lb ground beef
1 onion, diced
2 cloves garlic, minced
1 tsp all spice
1/2 tsp ground coriander
1/2 tsp ground cumin
Salt and pepper to taste

Instructions:
1. Preheat oven to 375 degrees F.
2. Heat a large skillet over medium heat and add the ground beef. Cook until browned, about 7-10 minutes.
3. Add the onions, garlic, all spice, coriander, cumin, salt and pepper to the skillet and mix all the Ingredients together.
4. Cut the puff pastry dough into 6 equal-size rectangles.
5. Fill each rectangle with some of the beef mixture and fold into triangles.
6. Place the sambusaks on a parchment-lined baking sheet and bake for 25 minutes or until golden brown.

Nutrition information: 270 calories, 12g fat, 26g carbs, 11g protein.

36. Burmuelos (Sephardic Donuts)

Burmuelo (Sephardic Donut) is an Eastern-style donut originating from Portugal and Spain with a crispy, golden exterior and soft, pillowy interior. It is a favorite among Sephardic-style Jewish cuisine.
Serving: 24 burmuelos
Preparation Time: 45 minutes
Ready Time: 2 hours

Ingredients:
- 4 cups all-purpose flour
- 2 teaspoons baking powder
- 2 teaspoons yeast
- 1 cup warm water

- 2/3 cup white sugar
- 2 eggs
- 1 teaspoon ground cinnamon
- 1/4 teaspoon ground nutmeg
- 1/2 teaspoon ground cardamom
- 1/4 teaspoon ground ginger
- 1/4 cup vegetable oil
- Oil for frying

Instructions:
1. In a large bowl, mix flour, baking powder, yeast, and sugar.
2. Add the warm water, eggs, cinnamon, nutmeg, cardamom, ginger, and vegetable oil to the dry Ingredients. Mix until a thick dough forms.
3. Cover the bowl with a towel and let the dough rise for 1 hour.
4. Once the dough is doubled in size, form into 24 small balls and place on a greased baking sheet.
5. Heat oil in a deep pan or fryer to 350°F.
6. Gently drop a few of the burmuelos into the hot oil and fry until golden brown, about 5 minutes per side.
7. Place on paper towels to drain excess oil and let cool slightly before serving.

Nutrition information:
Calories: 124 calories, Total Fat: 6.3g, Saturated Fat: 2.8g, Cholesterol: 27mg, Sodium: 31mg, Carbohydrates: 15.2g, Dietary Fiber: 0.9g, Sugars: 5.2g, Protein: 2.3g

37. Stuffed Grape Leaves

Stuffed Grape Leaves is a delicious and traditional dish originating from Greece and Turkey. It is made with grape leaves stuffed with a delicious vegetarian or meat filling, and then served with a variety of accompaniments.
Serving: 4-6
Preparation time: 20 minutes
Ready time: 60 minutes

Ingredients:

- 1/2 cup uncooked long-grain rice
- 2 tablespoons extra-virgin olive oil
- 1/2 cup finely chopped onion
- 1/2 cup finely chopped celery
- 1/2 cup finely chopped carrots
- 1/2 cup finely chopped mushrooms
- 1 teaspoon chopped fresh dill
- 1/2 teaspoon salt and freshly ground black pepper
- 1/2 cup feta cheese
- 1/4 cup dry white wine
- 2 jars of grape leaves

Instructions:
1. Preheat oven to 350°F.
2. In a large saucepan, over medium heat, add the rice, cover with water, and bring to a boil. Reduce heat to low and simmer for 15-20 minutes, or until water is absorbed and rice is tender.
3. In a large skillet, heat olive oil over medium heat. Add the onion, celery, carrots, mushrooms, dill, and salt and pepper. Cook for 5-7 minutes, or until vegetables are tender.
4. Remove from heat and stir in the feta cheese and rice.
5. Lay one of the jars of drained grape leaves on a cutting board. Place one grape leaf at a time in your hand and add a heaping tablespoon of the filling in the middle of each one. Fold up the sides of the grape leaf around the filling and close it up like a package.
6. Place the stuffed grape leaves side by side in an oven safe dish. Pour in the white wine.
7. Cover the dish with a snug fitting lid and bake for 35-40 minutes.

Nutrition information: Per Serving – 120 Calories; 5 g Fat; 1.5 g Saturated Fat; 6 g Protein; 12 g Carbohydrate; 1 g Dietary Fiber; 15 mg Cholesterol; 170 mg Sodium.

38. Shakshorit

Shakshorit is a traditional Moroccan dish of stewed chicken and vegetables, known for its tantalizing flavors and unique blend of herbs and spices. This tasty dish is easy to make and is a great option for a delicious family dinner or a gourmet meal.

Serving: 4
Preparation Time: 15 minutes
Ready Time: 45 minutes

Ingredients:
- 4 chicken thighs
- 2 cloves garlic, minced
- 2 medium onions, sliced
- 2 tablespoons olive oil
- 2 carrots, sliced
- 1 teaspoon freshly ground black pepper
- ½ teaspoon cumin
- ½ teaspoon turmeric
- ½ teaspoon paprika
- 2 tablespoons tomato paste
- 1 teaspoon salt
- Handful of chopped fresh parsley

Instructions:
1. Heat the olive oil in a large pan over medium heat.
2. Add the onions and sauté for 5 minutes or until beginning to soften.
3. Add the garlic, carrots, and spices and cook for 2 minutes longer.
4. Add the chicken thighs and cook for about 10 minutes, stirring occasionally until all sides of the chicken are lightly browned.
5. Add the tomato paste, salt, and 1 cup of water and stir to combine.
6. Cover the pan and reduce the heat to medium-low, and cook for about 25 minutes, stirring occasionally.
7. Once the chicken is cooked through and the vegetables are tender, add the chopped parsley, stir to combine, and turn off the heat.

Nutrition information: For each serving, with 2 tablespoons olive oil, it contains approximately 330 calories, 17 g fat, 2 g carbohydrates, and 43 g of protein.

39. Pomegranate Chicken

Pomegranate Chicken is a delicious, Persian-inspired dish made with tender chicken thighs braised in a spicy-sweet pomegranate sauce. This is the perfect dish to add some international flair to your weeknight dinner routine!
Serving: 4-6
Preparation time: 15 minutes
Ready Time: 1.5 hours

Ingredients:
- 4-6 boneless skinless chicken thighs
- 1/4 cup pomegranate molasses
- 1/2 cup chicken stock
- 2 cloves garlic, minced
- 1 teaspoon ground cumin
- 1 teaspoon ground coriander
- 1 teaspoon turmeric
- 2 tablespoons olive oil
- 1/4 cup pine nuts
- 1/4 cup fresh parsley, chopped

Instructions:
1. Preheat oven to 375°F. Grease a baking dish and set aside.
2. In a medium bowl, combine pomegranate molasses, chicken stock, garlic, cumin, coriander, turmeric, olive oil, and pine nuts.
3. Place chicken in baking dish and top with pomegranate mixture. Cover dish with aluminum foil and bake for 45 minutes.
4. Remove aluminum foil and bake uncovered for an additional 30 minutes, until chicken is cooked through and sauce is thick and bubbling.
5. Top with fresh parsley before serving.

Nutrition information
Per Serving: Calories: 336; Fat: 19g; Carbohydrates: 16g; Protein: 24g; Sodium: 343mg

40. Bourekas with Potato and Mushroom

Bourekas with Potato and Mushroom are make-ahead delicious stuffed pastries filled with a flavorful combination of potatoes and mushrooms.

They are perfect for appetizers, brunch, or as a side dish. Serving: 4-6 people Preparation Time: 45 minutes Ready Time: 1 hour

Ingredients:
1 sheet of store-bought puff pastry, thawed
1 cup cooked potatoes, mashed
1 cup mushrooms, chopped
1/2 teaspoon freshly ground black pepper
3 tablespoons vegetable oil

Instructions:
1. Pre-heat oven to 375F.
2. On a lightly floured work surface, roll out puff pastry to about 1/8-inch thick.
3. Cut the puff pastry into 2-inch squares.
4. In a medium bowl, combine potatoes, mushrooms, pepper, and oil until well blended.
5. Place 1 teaspoon of the potato and mushroom mixture onto each puff pastry square.
6. Fold one corner of the square into the center, and press it to the other corner to form a triangle. Crimp the edges tightly to seal the filling in.
7. Place the pastries onto a baking sheet and bake for 20-25 minutes, or until golden brown.
8. Serve warm.

Nutrition information: Calories per serving: 211, Carbohydrates: 16g, Protein: 3g, Fat: 14g.

41. Algerian Harira

Algerian Harira is a thick stew of beans, chickpeas, lentils and other vegetables, all seasoned with a mix of fragrant Middle Eastern spices. It's a hearty, comforting meal that's perfect for a cold winter evening and a great way to use up left-over veggies.
Serving: 4
Preparation Time: 10 minutes
Ready Time: 50 minutes

Ingredients:
- 2 cups cooked chickpeas
- 1 cup cooked lentils
- 1 onion, diced
- 2 cloves garlic, minced
- 1 can (14 ounces) diced tomatoes
- 2 tablespoons tomato paste
- 2 teaspoons ground cumin
- 2 teaspoons ground coriander
- 1 teaspoon paprika
- 1/2 teaspoon ground ginger
- 1 teaspoon salt
- 1/4 teaspoon ground black pepper
- 2 cups vegetable broth or water
- 2 cups chopped fresh vegetables of your choice (such as carrots, green beans, peppers or squash)
- 2 tablespoons chopped fresh cilantro
- 1/4 cup chopped fresh parsley

Instructions:
1. In a large pot, heat the olive oil over medium heat. Add the onions and garlic and cook for 5 minutes, until the onions are softened.
2. Add the tomatoes, tomato paste, cumin, coriander, paprika, ginger, salt, and pepper and stir to combine.
3. Add the vegetable broth or water, chickpeas, lentils, and chopped vegetables and simmer for 30 minutes. Stir in the cilantro and parsley and continue to simmer for 10 more minutes.
4. Taste and adjust the seasonings if desired. Serve hot with your favorite steamed grain or a crusty piece of bread.

Nutrition information:
Calories: 309, Fat: 4.6g, Carbs: 50.9g, Protein: 16.6g, Fiber: 11.9g

42. Cucumber and Tomato Salad

This light and refreshing Cucumber and Tomato Salad is a perfect side dish. Bursting with flavor, this simple salad is packed with vitamins and antioxidants.

Serving: 4
Preparation Time: 10 minutes
Ready Time: 10 minutes

Ingredients:
- 2 large tomatoes, cut into wedges
- 1 cucumber, chopped
- 2 tablespoons finely chopped fresh parsley
- 2 tablespoons olive oil
- 2 tablespoons red wine vinegar
- Salt and pepper, to taste

Instructions:
1. In a large salad bowl, combine the tomatoes, cucumber, and parsley.
2. In a separate small bowl, whisk together the olive oil and red wine vinegar.
3. Pour the olive oil and vinegar mixture over the salad Ingredients and season with salt and pepper, to taste.
4. Toss to combine then serve immediately.

Nutrition information: Calories: 141, Total Fat: 11 g, Saturated Fat: 1.5 g, Cholesterol: 0 mg, Sodium: 4 mg, Carbohydrates: 8 g, Fiber: 2 g, Sugars: 5 g, Protein: 2 g

43. Lamb Tajine with Prunes

Lamb Tajine with Prunes is a popular stew from the North African region, cooked with sweet prunes and spices, which provide a unique flavor. This dish is loaded with heart-healthy vegetables, making it a healthy, yet delicious option for everyone.
Serving: 6-8
Preparation time: 15 minutes
Ready time: 2 hours

Ingredients:
2 tablespoons olive oil
1 teaspoon cumin
1 teaspoon white pepper

2 onions, diced
2 garlic cloves, minced
2 pounds lamb, cut into cubes
2 teaspoons salt
2 tablespoons tomato paste
2 3-inch cinnamon sticks
2 cups chicken broth
2 cups pitted prunes

Instructions:
1. In a large pot, heat olive oil over medium-high heat.
2. Add cumin, pepper, onions, garlic, and lamb cubes, stirring occasionally until lightly browned.
3. Stir in salt, tomato paste, cinnamon sticks, and chicken broth.
4. Reduce heat to low and simmer, stirring occasionally, for 1 hour.
5. Add prunes and simmer for an additional 1 hour or until the lamb is tender.

Nutrition information (per serving): Calories: 376, Fat: 15g, Carbohydrates: 36g, Protein: 28g, Sodium: 1400mg

44. Malawach

Malawach is an Israeli flatbread that is crispy, light and fragrant. It has a unique texture and flavor that is sure to please everyone.
Serving: 4
Preparation Time: 15 minutes
Ready Time: 25 minutes

Ingredients:
-2 cups all-purpose flour
-1 teaspoon baking powder
-1 teaspoon salt
-1 cup warm water
-4 tablespoons vegetable oil

Instructions:
1. In a large bowl, mix together the flour, baking powder and salt.

2. Add the warm water and two tablespoons of the oil. Knead until a smooth dough is formed.

3. Shape the dough into a large ball and cover with a damp towel. Let it rest in a warm place for at least 15 minutes.

4. Preheat the oven to 375°F (190°C).

5. Divide the dough into four equal pieces and roll them out.

6. Heat a large heavy-based skillet over medium-high heat and add one tablespoon of oil. Place one rolled out piece of dough in the skillet and cook it until lightly golden and slightly crisp. Flip the dough and brown the other side.

7. Transfer the malawach to a baking sheet and repeat with the remaining three pieces. Bake the malawach for 10 minutes, or until slightly golden and crispy.

Nutrition information:
Calories: 302 kcal, Carbohydrates: 33 g, Protein: 4 g, Fat: 16 g, Saturated Fat: 12 g, Sodium: 477 mg, Potassium: 82 mg, Fiber: 1 g, Sugar: 1 g, Vitamin A: 4 IU, Calcium: 22 mg, Iron: 2 mg.

45. Kibbeh Nayeh

Kibbeh Nayeh is a traditional dish from the Middle East made with bulgur wheat and ground meat. It is usually prepared as a mezze starter dish, but can also be served as a main course. Kibbeh Nayeh is typically served raw, but can also be pan-fried or deep-fried.

Serving: Serves 6
Preparation Time: 30 minutes
Ready Time: 1 hour

Ingredients:
- 2 cups bulgur wheat
- 1 lb. ground meat (lamb or beef)
- 2 onions, chopped
- 1/4 cup olive oil
- 2 tablespoons ground cinnamon
- 1 teaspoon ground allspice
- Salt and freshly ground black pepper, to taste
- 2 tablespoons pine nuts

- 2 tablespoons chopped parsley

Instructions:
1. Soak the bulgur wheat in warm water for 30 minutes. Drain and squeeze out any excess water.
2. In a large bowl, mix together the bulgur wheat, ground meat, onions, olive oil, cinnamon, allspice, salt, and pepper.
3. Form the mixture into small balls (about golf-ball size) and place on a baking sheet.
4. Bake in a pre-heated 375F oven for 30 minutes, or until the meat is cooked through.
5. Garnish with pine nuts and parsley, and serve.

Nutrition information:
Calories: 348
Fat: 18g
Carbohydrates: 16g
Protein: 27g

46. Imam Bayildi

Imam bayildi is a classic Mediterranean dish of stuffed eggplant. Originating from the Ottoman Empire, the traditional dish features smoky roasted eggplant that is stuffed with a flavorful sautéed onion and tomato filling.
Serving: 4
Preparation time: 10 minutes
Ready time: 1 hour

Ingredients:
-4 medium eggplants
-4 tablespoons extra-virgin olive oil
-1 onion, finely chopped
-2 cloves garlic, minced
-1 teaspoon ground cumin
-1 teaspoon paprika
-1 (14.5 oz) can diced tomatoes
-2 tablespoons chopped fresh parsley

-2 tablespoons chopped fresh mint
-1 teaspoon sugar
-Salt and black pepper to taste

Instructions:
1. Preheat the oven to 375°F (190°C).
2. Cut the eggplants in half lengthwise. With a small knife, score the cut side of each eggplant half and season with salt and pepper.
3. Heat olive oil in a large skillet over medium heat. Add the onion and garlic and sauté for 5 minutes until softened. Add the cumin, paprika, tomatoes, parsley, mint, sugar and salt and pepper to taste. Simmer for 10 minutes, stirring occasionally.
4. Place the eggplant halves cut side up in a large baking dish. Divide the tomato sauce among the eggplant halves.
5. Bake for 45 minutes until the eggplant is tender.

Nutrition information:
Calories: 147 kcal, Carbohydrates: 17 g, Protein: 5 g, Fat: 9 g, Saturated Fat: 1 g, Sodium: 179 mg, Potassium: 652 mg, Fiber: 8 g, Sugar: 10 g, Vitamin A: 878 IU, Vitamin C: 27 mg, Calcium: 25 mg, Iron: 1 mg

47. Haminados (Slow-Cooked Eggs)

Haminados are a type of slow-cooked eggs which are deeply flavored and popular in traditional Ashkenazi Jewish cuisine. They can be served in sandwiches, with matzah, or as a side dish.
Serving: 4
Preparation time: 5 minutes
Ready time: 1 hour

Ingredients:
- 8 eggs
  1 onion, quartered
- 3 tablespoons vegetable oil
- 1 teaspoon paprika
- 1 teaspoon ground turmeric
- 2 to 3 cups water
- Salt and pepper, to taste

Instructions:
1. Preheat the oven to 350 degrees F (175 degrees C).
2. Place eggs in a baking dish. Arrange the onion around the eggs.
3. Drizzle vegetable oil over the eggs and onions. Sprinkle paprika and turmeric into the baking dish.
4. Pour the water into the dish until the eggs are mostly covered. Season with salt and pepper.
5. Cover the dish with a lid or aluminum foil.
6. Bake in the preheated oven for 1 hour.
7. Remove from the oven and let cool. Serve warm in sandwiches, with matzah, or as a side dish.

Nutrition information:
Calories: 136; Fat: 10.1g; Carbohydrates: 2g; Protein: 8g; Cholesterol: 186mg; Sodium: 104mg; Fiber: 0.1g.

48. Sephardic Fish Tagine

Sephardic Fish Tagine is a traditional Moroccan dish that features a variety of tasty Ingredients, including fish, peppers, tomatoes and a flavorful seasoning. It is a wonderful and delicious combination of flavors that will tantalize your taste buds.
Serving: Serves 4
Preparation time: 10 minutes
Ready time: 25 minutes

Ingredients:
-1½ lbs. firm white fish fillets
-1 onion, finely chopped
-2 cloves garlic, minced
-1 red bell pepper finely chopped
-1 green bell pepper finely chopped
-1 jalapeno pepper, seed and finely chopped
-1 bay leaf
-1/2 teaspoon ground ginger
-3 tablespoons olive oil
-1 cup diced tomatoes

-1/3 cup white cooking wine
-1 cup chicken broth
-1/2 teaspoon ground coriander
-1 teaspoon cumin
-1/4 teaspoon cinnamon
-1/4 teaspoon turmeric
-2 tablespoons chopped cilantro
-1/2 teaspoon paprika

Instructions:
1. Heat the olive oil in a large pot over medium heat. Add the onion, garlic, peppers, and jalapeno pepper, and cook for 5 minutes, or until the vegetables are softened.
2. Add the bay leaf, ginger, tomatoes, white wine, chicken broth, coriander, cumin, cinnamon, turmeric, cilantro, and paprika. Bring the mixture to a boil, then reduce the heat to low and simmer for 10 minutes.
3. Add the fish fillets to the pot, simmer for 10 minutes, or until the fish is cooked through. Serve over hot cooked rice or couscous.

Nutrition information:
Calories — 288
Fat — 9.2 g
Carbohydrates — 11.6 g
Protein — 32.5 g

49. Börek

Börek is a type of savory pastry made of thin layers of phyllo dough that are filled with cheese, ground beef or vegetables. It is a classic Turkish dish often served as an appetizer or snack.
Serving: 4
Preparation Time: 10 minutes
Ready Time: 20 minutes

Ingredients:
- 1 package of phyllo dough
- 2 cups of crumbled feta cheese
- 1/2 cup of melted butter

- 1/2 cup of chopped scallions or green onions (optional)
- 1 cup of finely chopped parsley (optional)

Instructions:
1. Preheat the oven to 375°F.
2. In a medium bowl, combine the crumbled feta cheese and chopped scallions or green onions (if desired).
3. Line a baking dish with half of the phyllo dough, brushing each sheet lightly with melted butter before adding the next one.
4. Spread the cheese mixture evenly over the phyllo and sprinkle with parsley (if desired).
5. Cover the cheese with the remaining phyllo dough and brush each sheet with melted butter before adding the next one.
6. Bake in the preheated oven for 20 minutes, or until golden brown.
7. Let cool for 10 minutes before serving.

Nutrition information: Not available.

50. Bulgarian Shopska Salad

Bulgarian Shopska Salad is a traditional dish from Bulgaria. Made of fresh vegetables, it's a healthy and delicious dish for the summer.
Serving: 4
Preparation time: 10 minutes
Ready time: 15 minutes

Ingredients:
• 2 cucumbers, diced
• 2 tomatoes, diced
• 1 green pepper, diced
• 1 onion, diced
• 4 ounces crumbled feta cheese
• 2 tablespoons fresh parsley, chopped
• ¼ cup olive oil
• 2 tablespoons white wine vinegar
• Salt and pepper to taste

Instructions:

1. In a large bowl, combine cucumbers, tomatoes, green pepper, onion, feta cheese, and parsley.
2. In a separate bowl, whisk together olive oil and vinegar. Pour over the vegetables and mix until all Ingredients are evenly coated.
3. Season with salt and pepper before serving.

Nutrition information:
Calories: 247, Fat: 22 g, Carbohydrates: 6 g, Protein: 5 g, Cholesterol: 34 mg, Sodium: 361 mg, Fiber: 2 g

51. Moroccan Chicken Tagine

Moroccan Chicken Tagine is a deliciously fragrant dish of chicken slow cooked in a variety of aromatic spices and vegetables.
Serving - 4-5
Preparation time - 10 minutes
Ready time - 40 minutes

Ingredients:
• 2 tablespoons olive oil
• 2 onions, finely chopped
• 2 cloves garlic, minced
• 2 teaspoons ground cumin
• 2 teaspoons ground ginger
• 1 teaspoon paprika
• ½ teaspoon turmeric
• ½ teaspoon cayenne pepper
• 1½ pounds boneless, skinless chicken thighs, cut into 1-inch cubes
• 1 can (14.5 ounces) diced tomatoes
• 1 cup chicken broth
• 1 can (15 ounces) chickpeas, rinsed and drained
• 2 carrots, peeled and diced
• 1 orange, zested and juiced
• 2 tablespoons chopped fresh cilantro

Instructions:
1. Heat the oil in a large Dutch oven over medium heat. Add the onions and garlic and cook until softened, about 4 minutes.

2. Add the cumin, ginger, paprika, turmeric, and cayenne and cook for 1 minute.

3. Add the chicken, tomatoes, broth, chickpeas, carrots, orange zest, and juice. Bring to a boil.

4. Reduce the heat to low, cover, and simmer until the chicken is cooked through and the vegetables are tender, about 30 minutes.

5. Garnish with cilantro.

Nutrition information - Per serving: Calories 327, Protein 25 g, Fat 15 g, Cholesterol 91 mg, Sodium 333 mg, Carbohydrates 18 g, Fiber 6 g

52. Lemony Chicken Soup

Satisfy your craving for something light but flavorful with this Lemony Chicken Soup. This delicious soup prepares in a flash, but its bright and lemony flavors make it taste like it was simmering all day!

Serving: 4

Preparation time: 10 minutes

Ready time: 30 minutes

Ingredients:
- 2 tablespoons olive oil
- 4 cloves garlic, minced
- 2 tablespoons fresh thyme, chopped
- 2 tablespoons all-purpose flour
- 6 cups chicken broth
- 1/4 teaspoon ground black pepper
- 2 cups cooked, diced chicken breast
- 1/2 cup uncooked small-shaped pasta
- 2 tablespoons lemon juice
- 1/4 cup Parmesan cheese, shredded

Instructions:
1. In a large saucepan over low heat, heat the oil and garlic for 3 minutes.
2. Add thyme and flour to the saucepan and cook for 2 minutes.
3. Add the chicken broth and bring to a boil.

4. Add the black pepper, chicken, and pasta and simmer for an additional 15 minutes, stirring occasionally.
5. Remove from heat and stir in the lemon juice.
6. Serve soup in individual bowls and top with Parmesan cheese.

Nutrition information: Calories: 368; Total fat: 16.3g; Saturated fat: 4.5g; Cholesterol: 87mg; Sodium: 730 mg; Carbohydrates: 21.4g; Fiber: 0.9g; Protein: 33.2g

53. Stuffed Peppers

This recipe for Stuffed Peppers offers a delicious combination of mushrooms, onions, and bell peppers with a hint of tomato sauce and grated cheese. It's a great side dish or main course that your family will love!
Serving: 4
Preparation Time: 15 minutes
Ready Time: 40 minutes

Ingredients:
- 4 bell peppers - any color
- 2 tablespoons olive oil
- 1 onion, diced
- 1 cup mushrooms, diced
- Salt and Pepper, to taste
- 1 cup cooked rice
- 1 (15 oz) can diced tomatoes
- 1 cup grated cheese

Instructions:
1. Preheat oven to 375 degrees.
2. Cut the bell peppers in half and remove the seeds and stems.
3. Place the peppers in a shallow baking dish.
4. In a large skillet, heat oil over medium-high heat. Add the onions and mushrooms and cook for 4-5 minutes until softened.
5. Add the rice, tomatoes, salt and pepper, and cook for another 3-4 minutes.

6. Fill the pepper halves with the rice mixture and top with the grated cheese.

7. Place the peppers in the oven for 20-30 minutes until the peppers are cooked through and the cheese is melted and bubbly.

Nutrition information:
Serving size: 1 half pepper
Calories: 185
Total fat: 8g
Cholesterol: 20mg
Sodium: 192mg
Carbohydrate: 21g
Fiber: 2g
Sugar: 4g
Protein: 8g

54. Brik

Brik is a traditional Tunisian pastry whose main components are filo dough stuffed with a mixture of egg, tuna, and onions. This dish is crunchy on the outside and juicy on the inside, delivering a unique blend of flavors and textures with every bite.
Serving: 4-6
Preparation time: 25 minutes
Ready time: 50 minutes

Ingredients:
- 6 sheets of filo dough
- 2 large eggs
- 2 cans of tuna, drained and mashed
- 1 onion, chopped
- 2 tablespoons of lemon juice
- 2 tablespoons of parsley, finely chopped
- 3/4 cup of vegetable oil
- Salt and pepper to taste

Instructions:
1. Preheat oven to 375°F (190°C).

2. In a bowl, beat together the eggs, tuna, onion, lemon juice, parsley, and salt and pepper.
3. Place a sheet of filo dough in a shallow baking dish and brush with vegetable oil.
4.Repeat this step with five remaining sheets of filo dough, brushing each one with oil.
5. Spread the tuna mixture over the top layer of filo dough and spread evenly.
6.Fold up the edges and brush the top with oil.
7.Bake for 30 minutes in preheated oven or until the filling is golden brown.
8.Allow to cool before cutting and serving.

Nutrition information:
Calories per serving: 425 kcal
Protein: 21.5 g
Carbs: 27.2 g
Fat: 19.8 g

55. Greek Spanakopita

Greek Spanakopita is a popular Greek dish, made from crispy layers of phyllo dough filled with a delicious combination of spinach, feta cheese, and herbs. It is an easy-to-make and light dish, that makes a perfect meal for any occasion.
Serving: 8
Preparation Time: 10 minutes
Ready Time: 40 minutes

Ingredients:
• 4 tablespoons butter, melted
• 1/2 cup onion, finely chopped
• 2 cloves garlic, minced
• 2 (10 ounce) packages chopped frozen spinach, thawed and drained
• 1 cup feta cheese, crumbled
• 1/4 cup chopped fresh parsley
• 1/4 cup chopped fresh dill
• 1/4 teaspoon salt

- 1/2 teaspoon ground black pepper
- 1/4 teaspoon ground nutmeg
- 8 sheets phyllo dough

Instructions:
1. Preheat oven to 350 degrees F (175 degrees C).
2. In a medium skillet over medium heat, cook onion and garlic in the melted butter until softened.
3. In a large bowl, mix together the cooked onion, garlic, spinach, feta cheese, parsley, dill, salt, pepper and nutmeg. Set aside.
4. Grease a 9x13 inch baking dish. Unroll the phyllo dough, and cut it to fit the dish. Layer 5 sheets of dough in the greased dish, brushing each sheet with butter before adding the next.
5. Spread the spinach mixture evenly over the dough. Top with remaining 3 sheets of dough, brushing each sheet with butter before adding the next.
6. Bake in preheated oven for 35 to 40 minutes, until golden brown.

Nutrition information: Nutrition information per serving: 420 calories; 15.1g fat; 55.6g carbohydrates; 11.4g protein; 46mg cholesterol; 522mg sodium.

56. Bimuelos (Fried Dough Balls)

Bimuelos (Fried Dough Balls) are a delicious fried dough treat that are popular throughout the Caribbean. Served between meals, as a breakfast item, or dessert, this fried dough is perfect when paired with your favorite dipping sauce!
Serving: 4
Preparation time: 20 minutes
Ready time: 45 minutes

Ingredients:
- 2 cups all-purpose flour
- 1 teaspoon baking powder
- 1 teaspoon salt
- 2 tablespoons sugar
- 1/4 cup vegetable oil

- 1/2 cup cold water
- Vegetable oil for frying

Instructions:
1. In a large mixing bowl, combine the flour, baking powder, salt and sugar and mix until well combined.
2. Pour the vegetable oil and cold water into the dry mixture and mix until a soft dough forms.
3. Turn the dough onto a lightly floured surface and knead until a smooth, elastic dough forms.
4. Divide the dough into 4 equal sized pieces and roll each piece into a rope about 1 1/2 to 2 inches thick.
5. Cut the dough rope into 2 inch pieces and set aside.
6. Heat the vegetable oil in a deep skillet or Dutch oven over medium-high heat.
7. Fry the dough pieces for about 2 minutes per side or until they are golden brown and cooked through.
8. Transfer the dough pieces to a paper towel lined plate to remove any excess oil.

Nutrition information:
Serving Size: 4 servings
Calories: 306 kcal
Total Fat: 15 g
Saturated Fat: 5 g
Total Carbohydrates: 35 g
Protein: 6 g

57. Armenian Lahmajun

Armenian lahmajun is a delectable flatbread-like pizza topped with a rich and flavorful ground beef and vegetable mixture. This delicious dish is sure to tantalize your taste-buds!
Serving: 4 servings
 Preparation Time: 5 minutes
Ready Time: 20 minutes

Ingredients:

- 1 package pre-made dough
- 1 onion, minced
- 1/4 cup parsley, chopped
- 2 cloves garlic, minced
- 1 lb ground beef
- 2 tomatoes, chopped
- Salt and pepper, to taste

Instructions:
1. Preheat oven to 425°F.
2. In a large bowl, combine onion, parsley, garlic, ground beef, tomatoes, salt, and pepper. Mix until combined.
3. Spread dough onto two non-stick baking sheets.
4. Divide the meat mixture into four equal portions and spread each portion onto the dough.
5. Put the baking sheets in the oven and bake for 20 minutes, or until the crust is lightly golden brown.
6. Serve hot.

Nutrition information: 1 serving (1/4 of the recipe) has 182 calories, 8 g total fat, 26 g carbohydrates, and 12 g protein.

58. Fasolada

Fasolada is a traditional Greek bean stew, typically consisting of white beans, garlic, celery, onions, tomato, olive oil, and herbs like parsley and oregano. This hearty and warming stew is easy to make and requires very few Ingredients.
Serving: 4-6
Preparation Time: 10 minutes
Ready Time: 2 hours

Ingredients:
- 2-3 tablespoons olive oil
- half a large onion, chopped
- 2 cloves garlic, minced
- 2-3 celery stalks, chopped
- 2 x 14-ounce cans white beans– drained and rinsed

- 2-3 cups vegetable or chicken broth
- 3 tablespoons tomato paste
- 2 tablespoons dried oregano
- 1 teaspoon dried parsley
- Salt and pepper, to taste

Instructions:
1. Heat oil in a large pot over medium heat.
2. Add onion and garlic and cook until softened, about 5 minutes.
3. Add celery and cook for an additional 2 minutes.
4. Add beans, broth, tomato paste, oregano, and parsley and stir well.
5. Bring to a boil, reduce heat, and simmer for 1.5-2 hours, or until the stew has thickened and the beans are tender.
6. Season with salt and pepper to taste.
7. Serve hot with a garnish of fresh parsley, if desired.

Nutrition information:
- Calories: 246
- Total Fat: 6.5 g
- Saturated Fat: 1 g
- Cholesterol: 0 mg
- Sodium: 444 mg
- Total Carbohydrates: 33.5 g
- Dietary Fiber: 11.5 g
- Sugar: 4.5 g
- Protein: 11.5 g

59. Spicy Harissa Chicken

Spicy Harissa Chicken is a unique combination of flavorful herbs such as cumin, paprika, garlic, hot peppers and harissa. It is a delicious dish that can be served over freshly cooked couscous.
Serving: 4
Preparation Time: 20 minutes
Ready Time: 45 minutes

Ingredients:
• 2 tablespoons extra-virgin olive oil

- 1½ pounds boneless and skinless chicken thighs
- 1 onion, chopped
- 2 garlic cloves, minced
- 2 tablespoons harissa paste
- 1 teaspoon cumin
- ½ teaspoon paprika
- ½ teaspoon kosher salt
- 1 (15-ounce) can diced tomatoes
- ¼ cup chopped fresh parsley

Instructions:
1. Heat oil in a large skillet over medium heat. Add chicken and cook for 6 minutes per side, until cooked through. Transfer chicken to a plate and set aside.
2. Add onions and garlic and cook for about 3 minutes, until softened. Stir in harissa, cumin, paprika and salt.
3. Return chicken to the skillet and add tomatoes. Bring to a simmer and cook for additional 10 minutes, stirring occasionally.
4. Remove from heat and stir in parsley.

Nutrition information (per serving): Calories: 270, Total Fat: 14g, Saturated Fat: 3g, Protein: 29g, Carbohydrates: 8g, Fiber: 1g, Sodium: 460mg

60. Halva

Halva is a traditional Middle Eastern dessert that is often made of semolina, flour, or nut butter. It is often served as a sweet after-meal treat or snack. It is a favorite in many cultures and is classified as a form of confectionary.
Serving: 4
Preparation Time: 10 minutes
Ready Time: 30 minutes

Ingredients:
· 1 cup tahini
· 1/2 cup honey
· 1/2 cup sugar

· 1/2 teaspoon ground cardamom
· 3 tablespoons olive oil
· 3/4 cup water

Instructions:
1. Heat the olive oil in a large pan over medium heat.
2. Add the tahini and stir until the tahini is melted and bubbly.
3. Add the honey and sugar and mix well.
4. Add the cardamom and mix for 1 minute until combined.
5. Turn the heat to low and slowly add the water, stirring constantly.
6. Cook for 10-15 minutes, stirring constantly, until thick and creamy.
7. Remove from heat and let cool for 10-15 minutes before serving.

Nutrition information:
Calories: 225, Fat: 14g, Saturated Fat: 2g, Trans Fat: 0g, Cholesterol: 0mg, Sodium: 4mg, Carbohydrates: 22g, Fiber: 2g, Sugar: 15g, Protein: 5g

61. Spicy Chraime Fish

Spicy Chraime Fish is a Middle-Eastern dish with a kick of spice that is usually served over couscous.
Serving: This dish serves 4 people.
Preparation time: 15 minutes
Ready Time: 40 minutes

Ingredients:
- 4 firm fish steaks
- 1 tablespoon olive oil
- 1 onion, finely chopped
- 2 cloves of garlic, chopped
- 2 tablespoon tomato puree
- 2 teaspoon dried chili flakes
  2 teaspoon paprika
- 1 teaspoon ground cumin
- 1 teaspoon ground coriander
- 1 teaspoon sugar
- Salt and pepper to taste
- 100 ml vegetable stock

- 100 ml dry white wine

Instructions:
1. Place the fish steaks onto an oven tray and then season with salt and pepper.
2. Heat the oil in a medium-sized saucepan on medium heat and add the onion, sauté until the onion has softened.
3. Add the garlic, tomato puree, chili flakes, paprika, cumin, coriander and sugar and mix until combined.
4. Pour the stock and wine into the saucepan and bring it to a simmer.
5. Place the fish steaks into an oven tray and pour the hot sauce over the fish.
6. Bake in a preheated oven at 190°C for 30 minutes.
7. When done, serve hot with couscous and your favorite vegetables.

Nutrition information
Per serving: 492 calories, 15g fat, 16g carbohydrates, 32g protein.

62. Revani (Semolina Cake)

Revani (Semolina Cake) is a classic Greek dessert that's dense, yet spongy, and mildly sweet. Served everywhere from cafés to home tables, it's sure to be a crowd pleaser for any sweet-tooth.
Serving: 6
Preparation Time: 25 minutes
Ready Time: 55 minutes

Ingredients:
- 2 cups semolina
- 2 cups all-purpose flour
- 2 cups sugar
- 4 teaspoons baking powder
- Zest of 1 lemon
- A pinch of salt
- 2 cups vegetable oil
- 2¾ cups whole milk
- 2 teaspoons vanilla extract
- ½ cup granulated sugar

Instructions:
1. Preheat oven to 350°F (177°C). Grease a 10-inch springform pan.
2. In a large bowl, sift together the semolina flour, all-purpose flour, sugar, baking powder, and salt.
3. Once combined, add in the oil, milk and vanilla extract and whisk everything together until combined.
4. Pour the mixture into the greased pan and bake in the preheated oven for approximately 35 minutes.
5. Remove from the oven and let cool. Prepare a simple syrup with a half cup of granulated sugar and a cup of warm water. Once cake is cooled, pour the syrup evenly over the top, letting it seep into the spongy texture.
6. Sprinkle the lemon zest over the top and serve.

Nutrition information:
Serving Size: 1 slice | Calories: 467 kcal | Fat: 21g | Saturated Fat: 10g | Sodium: 211mg | Carbohydrates: 60g | Fiber: 2g | Sugar: 32g | Protein: 8g

63. Tunisian Shakshouka

Tunisian Shakshouka is a classic dish, enriched with spicy tomatoes, onions, garlic, and flavorful herbs. Perfect as breakfast, dinner, or lunch, this one-pan dish is sure to bring delight to any dining table.
Serving: 6
Preparation time: 15 minutes
Ready time: 25 minutes

Ingredients:
- 1 large onion, diced small
- 2 tablespoons oil
  2 cloves garlic, minced
- 1 red bell pepper, diced
- 1 jalapeno, minced
- 1 teaspoon smoked paprika
- 2 teaspoons Moroccan seasoning
- ¼ teaspoon cayenne pepper

- 1 tablespoon tomato paste
- 2 (14.5 ounce) cans diced tomatoes
- ½ teaspoon sugar
- 6 eggs
- Salt and pepper, to taste
- Chopped parsley, for garnish

Instructions:
1. Heat the oil in a large skillet over medium heat.
2. Add the onion and bell pepper and cook for 2 minutes, stirring occasionally.
3. Add the garlic, jalapeño, paprika, Moroccan seasoning, cayenne pepper, and tomato paste. Cook for 1 minute, stirring constantly.
4. Add the diced tomatoes and sugar. Cook for 8 minutes, stirring occasionally.
5. Reduce the heat to low and crack the eggs one at a time over the sauce. Cover the skillet and cook for 10 minutes.
6. Season the shakshouka with salt and pepper to taste.
7. Sprinkle with parsley and serve.

Nutrition information: Per Serving: 370 calories, 16.5 g fat, 6.9 g protein, 40.0 g carbohydrate, 5.5 g dietary fiber, 465 mg sodium.

64. Greek Moussaka

Greek Moussaka is an eggplant and ground meat casserole that is seasoned with Mediterranean spices and topped with a creamy béchamel sauce.
Serving: Serves 6
Preparation time: 25 minutes
Ready time: 65 minutes

Ingredients:
- 2 pounds ground beef
- 1 large yellow onion, finely diced
- 6 cloves garlic, minced
- 2 tablespoons tomato paste
- 1 teaspoon ground cinnamon

- 1 teaspoon dry oregano
- 1/2 teaspoon ground nutmeg
- 2 teaspoons paprika
- 1 teaspoon allspice
- Salt and pepper to taste
- 2 large eggplants, sliced
- 4 tablespoons olive oil
- 1 cup dry red wine
- 2 (15-ounce) cans crushed tomatoes
- 4 tablespoons butter
- 4 tablespoons all-purpose flour
- 2 cups milk
- 1/2 cup grated Parmesan cheese

Instructions:
1. Preheat oven to 375 degrees F.
2. In a large skillet over medium heat, cook the beef, onion, garlic, tomato paste, cinnamon, oregano, nutmeg, paprika, and allspice for about 10 minutes, stirring occasionally until the beef is browned.
3. Meanwhile, prepare the eggplant slices by brushing each side lightly with olive oil and seasoning with salt and pepper.
4. Place a layer of eggplant on the bottom of a greased 9x13-inch baking dish.
5. Top with the beef mixture and then place another layer of eggplant slices over the beef.
6. Pour the wine over the top and then spread the crushed tomatoes over the eggplant.
7. Bake for 30 minutes.
8. While the dish is cooking, prepare the béchamel sauce. In a saucepan over medium heat, melt butter and add the flour, stirring for 1 minute.
9. Slowly pour in the milk, whisking constantly until the sauce is thick and creamy.
10. Stir in Parmesan cheese and remove from heat.
11. Once the moussaka is finished baking, spread béchamel sauce over the top of the dish and bake for an additional 20 minutes.

Nutrition information: Per serving: 630 calories, 34 g fat (14 g saturated fat, 4 g polyunsaturated fat, 11 g monounsaturated fat), 135 mg cholesterol, 583 mg sodium, 18 g carbohydrates, 2 g fiber, 5 g sugar, 38 g protein.

65. Fasolia

Fasolia is a classic Mediterranean and Middle Eastern stew made with beans, tomatoes, onions, and garlic. It is a one-pot meal packed with flavour and nutrition, and it can be served over rice, as a dipping sauce for bread, or on its own.

Serving: 4-6
Preparation Time: 15 minutes
Ready Time: 55 minutes

Ingredients:
- 1 tablespoon olive oil
- 1 large onion, diced
- 1 garlic clove, minced
- 1 cup canned diced tomatoes
- 2 cups cooked white beans
- 2 cups vegetable broth
- 1 teaspoon dried oregano
- 1 teaspoon dried thyme
- 1 teaspoon ground cumin
- Salt and pepper, to taste
- ¼ cup fresh parsley, chopped

Instructions:
1. Heat the olive oil in a large pot over medium heat.
2. Add the onion and garlic and cook until soft, about 5 minutes.
3. Add the canned tomatoes and cook for another 5 minutes.
4. Add the beans, broth, oregano, thyme, and cumin. Bring to a boil, then reduce heat and simmer for 30 minutes.
5. Taste and season with salt and pepper, if needed.
6. Stir in the parsley and serve.

Nutrition information:
Calories: 188, Total Fat: 4g, Saturated Fat: 1g, Cholesterol: 0mg, Sodium: 498mg, Total Carbohydrates: 28g, Protein: 5g, Fiber: 6g.

66. Sultan's Delight

Sultan's Delight is a rich and exotic Middle Eastern sweet dish typically served at special occasions.
Serving: 10
Preparation time: 45 minutes
Ready time: 1 hour

Ingredients:
- 2 cups ground walnuts
- 2 cups dates, pitted and chopped
- 1 teaspoon ground cinnamon
- 2 tablespoons butter, melted
- ½ teaspoon nutmeg
- 1 tablespoon cardamom
- 2 tablespoons almond extract
- 2 tablespoons honey
- 1 tablespoon orange blossom water
- 1 teaspoon rose water

Instructions:
1. Preheat oven to 350°F.
2. In a medium bowl, mix together walnuts, dates, cinnamon, melted butter, nutmeg, cardamom, almond extract, honey, orange blossom water, and rose water.
3. Spread the mixture into a 9x13-inch baking dish.
4. Bake in preheated oven for 30 to 40 minutes, or until golden brown.
5. Serve warm or chilled.

Nutrition information:
- Calories: 150
- Total fat: 8g
- Cholesterol: 0mg
- Sodium: 7mg
- Total carbohydrates: 17g
- Protein: 3g

67. Cabbage Rolls

Cabbage Rolls are a classic Eastern European dish full of delicious and savory flavors. This hearty dish consists of cabbage leaves stuffed with ground beef and cooked in a fragrant tomato sauce. Rich in nutrition and sure to please crowds, this is a delicious dish you don't want to miss!

Serving: 4

Preparation time: 25 minutes

Ready time: 1 hour 30 minutes

Ingredients:
- 1 large head of green cabbage
- 1 lb. ground beef
- 1/2 cup of uncooked, white rice
- 2 cloves of garlic, minced
- 1 small onion, minced
- 1 teaspoon of dried oregano
- 1/2 teaspoon of paprika
- 1/2 teaspoon of ground black pepper
- Salt to taste
- 1 15-ounce can of tomato sauce

Instructions:
1. Preheat oven to 350 degrees.
2. Bring a large pot of water to a boil. Core the cabbage and break the leaves off one at a time. Place the leaves in the boiling water and blanch them for 5 minutes or until softened. Drain the leaves and set them aside.
3. In a bowl, combine the ground beef, rice, garlic, onion, oregano, paprika, black pepper and salt. Mix well.
4. Place a cabbage leaf on a clean surface and place a small amount of the beef mixture in the center of the leaf. Roll the leaf up, tucking in the sides as you roll it. Secure the roll with one or two toothpicks. Repeat until all of the flling is used up.
5. Place the cabbage rolls in an oven-safe baking dish. Pour the tomato sauce over them and cover the dish with aluminum foil.
6. Bake for 1 hour and 15 minutes, or until the cabbage rolls are cooked through.

Nutrition information: Per serving (4 servings): Calories: 332 Fat: 6.7g Carbs: 41.2g Protein: 27.8g

68. Turlu

Turlu is a traditional Turkish vegetable stew made with fresh seasonal vegetables. It is often served as part of a larger shared meal.
Serving: 6
Preparation Time: 20 minutes
Ready Time: 45 minutes

Ingredients:
• 2 cups of diced onion
• 2 tablespoons of minced garlic
• 5 to 6 fresh tomatoes, diced
• 2 cups of diced eggplant
• 3 potatoes, diced
• 2 sweet peppers, diced
• 1/2 cup of olive oil
• 2 tablespoons of tomato paste
• 1 teaspoon of sugar
• Salt and pepper to taste

Instructions:
1. Heat the olive oil in a Dutch oven over medium heat.
2. Add the onions and garlic to the Dutch oven and cook until softened, about 5 minutes.
3. Add the tomatoes and cook for another 5 minutes.
4. Add the eggplant, potatoes, sweet peppers, tomato paste, and sugar.
5. Season with salt and pepper to taste.
6. Cover the Dutch oven and cook for 25 minutes, or until the vegetables are cooked through.
7. Serve warm.

Nutrition information: Per serving: 159 calories; 9.4 g fat; 16.9 g carbohydrates; 2.4 g protein; 10 mg cholesterol; 216 mg sodium.

69. Turkish Pilaf

Turkish Pilaf is a classic rice dish that is full of flavor and makes for a satisfying side dish or main course. It is a popular dish throughout Turkey and the Middle East, made with long-grain rice, vegetables, and spices.

Serving: 8
Preparation Time: 15 minutes
Ready Time: 45 minutes

Ingredients:
- 2 tablespoons olive oil
- 1 onion, minced
- 4 garlic cloves, minced
- 1 cup diced carrots
- 2 cups long-grain white rice
- 2 cups chicken broth or vegetable broth
- 2 teaspoons paprika
- 1 teaspoon dried oregano
- ½ teaspoon ground cumin
- ½ teaspoon ground coriander
- ½ teaspoon ground allspice
- 1 bay leaf
- Salt to taste

Instructions:
1. Heat the oil in a large pot over medium heat.
2. Add the onion and garlic and sauté for 2 minutes.
3. Add the carrots and sauté for another 2 minutes.
4. Add the rice and sauté for 2 more minutes.
5. Add the broth, paprika, oregano, cumin, coriander, allspice, and bay leaf.
6. Season with salt to taste.
7. Bring to a boil, reduce heat to low, cover, and simmer for 20-25 minutes or until the liquid has been absorbed and the rice is cooked through.
8. Serve hot.

Nutrition Information (per serving):

Calories: 161, Fat: 4.9g, Saturated fat: 0.7g, Carbohydrate: 26.4g, Fiber: 1.9g, Protein: 3.3g

70. Moroccan Bastilla

Moroccan Bastilla is a traditional Moroccan pie made with fillopastry, savory filling of shredded meat and almonds, and a sweet, crunchy topping of toasted almonds and cinnamon. It's a flavorful, unique dish that's sure to please your guests.
Serving: 8 servings
Preparation time: 25 minutes
Ready time: 2 hours

Ingredients:
- 2 cups minced or finely chopped cooked chicken
- 2 tablespoons butter
- 1 onion, chopped
- 1 tablespoon cinnamon
- 1 teaspoon ground ginger
- 1 teaspoon ground black pepper
- 1/4 teaspoon ground nutmeg
- 2 tablespoons chopped fresh parsley
- Salt to taste
- 4 tablespoons olive oil
- 1/2 cup blanched almonds
- 20 sheets filo pastry
- 2 tablespoons melted butter
- 2 tablespoons slivered almonds

Instructions:
1. Preheat oven to 350°F (176°C).
2. Heat the butter in a skillet over medium heat. Add onion and cook until softened, about 5 minutes.
3. Add chicken, cinnamon, ginger, pepper, nutmeg, parsley, and salt to skillet and cook until chicken is heated through.
4. Spread olive oil over a 9x13-inch baking dish.
5. Layer the filo sheets in the baking dish, brushing each with melted butter and sprinkling with blanched almonds.

6. Spread chicken mixture over the top of the pastry.
7. Place remaining filo sheets over the top, again brushing each with melted butter and sprinkling with slivered almonds.
8. Bake for 25 minutes or until golden brown.

Nutrition information: Each serving contains 440 calories, 22g of fat, 31g of carbohydrates, 25g of protein, and 1g of dietary fiber.

71. Grilled Halloumi

Grilled Halloumi is a delicious Mediterranean style cheese made of sheep and goat milk. It's savory and salty flavor when cooked makes it a great addition to salads, sandwiches, and many other dishes. It's easy to prepare and is sure to become a favorite for lunch or dinner.
Serving: 4
Preparation Time: 5 minutes
Ready Time: 10 minutes

Ingredients:
- 500g Halloumi
- Olive oil

Instructions:
1. Slice the halloumi into thick slices.
2. Grease a pan with the olive oil.
3. Place the halloumi slices in the pan and cook for 5 minutes over medium heat.
4. Flip the slices and cook for another 5 minutes until they are golden brown.
5. Serve warm and enjoy.

Nutrition information: (per serving)
Calories: 190
Fat: 13g
Carbohydrates: 1g
Protein: 17g

72. Egyptian Kushari

Egyptian Kushari is a popular street dish that consists of a delightful combination of fried onions, lentils, macaroni and rice. The dish is topped with a tomato and garlic sauce and a spicy vinegar mixture.
Serves: 4 Preparation time: 25 minutes Ready time: 50 minutes

Ingredients:
• 1 onion, chopped • 1 teaspoon of oil • 1 cup of lentils, cooked • 2 cups of cooked macaroni • 2 cups of rice • 2 tablespoons of tomato sauce • 2 tablespoons of garlic paste • 1 tablespoon of vinegar • 2 bay leaves • 2 tablespoons of chili flakes • Salt and pepper

Instructions:
1. In a large saucepan, heat the oil over medium heat and then add the onions. Cook for 5-7 minutes, stirring occasionally.
2. After the onions have softened, add the cooked lentils, macaroni and rice, tomato sauce, garlic paste, vinegar, bay leaves, chili flakes, salt and pepper. Mix everything together.
3. Cover the saucepan and let the mixture simmer for 25 minutes, stirring occasionally.
4. Once the mixture has cooked, turn off the heat and let it rest for 5 minutes.
5. Serve the Egyptian Kushari warm. Nutrition information:
Calories: 297, Total Fat: 2g, Saturated Fat: 0g, Cholesterol: 0mg, Sodium: 82mg, Total Carbohydrate: 56g, Dietary Fiber: 11g, Sugar: 3g, Protein: 11g.

73. Taboon Bread

Taboon bread is a traditional Middle Eastern flatbread that is cooked in a stone oven and served with a variety of savory dips or toppings. It is full of flavor and is incredibly versatile.
Serving: Makes 6 flatbreads
Preparation time: 25 minutes
Ready time: 40 minutes

Ingredients:

2 cups bread flour (plus extra for dusting)
1 teaspoon table salt
1 teaspoon sugar
1/2 teaspoon active dry yeast
3/4 cup plus 2 tablespoons warm water

Instructions:
1. In a large bowl combine the flour, salt, sugar, and yeast.
2. Add the warm water and mix until a dough forms. Knead for 5 minutes.
3. Place the dough in a large, greased bowl and cover with a damp cloth. Let rise for 30 minutes.
4. Preheat oven to 500 degrees.
5. Divide the dough into 6 pieces and roll each piece into a thin round.
6. Place each piece of dough on a greased baking sheet. Bake for 8 minutes, or until lightly browned.

Nutrition information:
Per Serving: 210 Calories, 2.5g Fat, 38g Carbs, 5g Protein.

74. Pomegranate Molasses Chicken

This delicious recipe combines tart pomegranate molasses, chicken, and fragrant spices to create a lightly sweet and zesty meal. This pomegranate molasses chicken is sure to be a hit with the entire family.
Serving: 4-6
Preparation Time: 10 minutes
Ready Time: 40 minutes

Ingredients:
- 4-5 chicken thighs
- 2 tablespoons olive oil
- 2 tablespoons pomegranate molasses
- 2 tablespoons white wine
- 2 tablespoons honey
- 1 teaspoon cumin
- 1 teaspoon garlic powder
- 1 teaspoon paprika

- 1 teaspoon cinnamon
- 1 teaspoon ground black pepper
- Salt, to taste

Instructions:
1. Preheat the oven to 375 degrees Fahrenheit.
2. In a large bowl, combine the olive oil, pomegranate molasses, white wine, honey, cumin, garlic powder, paprika, cinnamon, and pepper.
3. Season the chicken thighs with salt, and then place the chicken thighs in the bowl with the marinade. Cover the chicken and marinade with plastic wrap and set aside for at least 10 minutes.
4. Place the marinated chicken thighs on a baking sheet.
5. Bake in the preheated oven for approximately 30 minutes.
6. Serve hot and enjoy.

Nutrition information:
Total Calories: Approx. 400 calories
Fat (per thigh): Approx. 24g
Carbohydrates (per thigh): Approx. 17g
Protein (per thigh): Approx. 23g

75. Koshari

Koshari is a unique and flavorful dish made with rice, macaroni, lentils, and chickpeas in an onion and garlic tomato-based sauce. It's packed with flavor and it's a popular dish throughout the Middle East.
Serving: Makes 4 - 6 servings
Preparation time: 20 minutes
Ready Time: 1 hour

Ingredients:
- 2 cups white long grain rice
- 1 cup uncooked macaroni
- 1 cup uncooked brown lentils
- 1 large onion, chopped
- 2 cloves garlic, minced
- 2 tablespoons olive oil
- 4 cups vegetable broth

- 1 (14.5 ounce) can diced tomatoes
- 2 teaspoons ground cumin
- 2 teaspoons paprika
- 1 teaspoon ground coriander
- 2 teaspoons kosher salt
- 1/2 teaspoon ground black pepper
- 1 (15 ounce) can chickpeas, drained

Instructions:
1. Preheat oven to 350°F.
2. Grease a 9x13 inch baking dish.
3. In a medium bowl, combine rice, macaroni, lentils, onion, garlic, olive oil, vegetable broth, diced tomatoes, cumin, paprika, coriander, salt, and pepper. Mix until combined.
4. Pour mixture into the prepared baking dish.
5. Bake for 30 minutes.
6. Remove from oven and stir in chickpeas.
7. Cover and bake for an additional 30 minutes.

Nutrition information
ServingSize 1.0 cup, Calories 385, Total Fat 4.5 g, Cholesterol 0 mg, Sodium 640 mg, Potassium 525 mg, Total Carbohydrates 75 g, Dietary Fiber 10 g, Sugars 8 g, Protein 12 g

76. Sephardic Couscous

Sephardic couscous is a delicious and traditional Mediterranean dish made with fluffy couscous, tender vegetables, and savory seasonings.
Serving: 6
Preparation Time: 10 minutes
Ready Time: 30 minutes

Ingredients:
-1 ½ cups prepared Israeli or pearl couscous
-3 tablespoons olive oil
-3 cloves garlic, minced
-1 teaspoon paprika
-2 tablespoons tomato paste

-½ teaspoon ground cumin
-3 cups vegetable broth
-1 onion, chopped
-2 carrots, chopped
-2 stalks celery, chopped
-1 zucchini, chopped
-1 red bell pepper, chopped
-1 cup peas
-2 tablespoons chopped fresh parsley
-Salt and pepper to taste

Instructions:
1. Heat the olive oil in a large saucepan over medium heat and add the garlic. Cook until fragrant, about 1 minute.
2. Add the paprika, tomato paste, and cumin and cook for another minute.
3. Add the vegetable broth and bring to a boil.
4. Add the couscous, onion, carrots, celery, zucchini, bell pepper, peas, and parsley. Reduce the heat to low and simmer until the vegetables are tender, about 20 minutes.
5. Season with salt and pepper to taste and serve.

Nutrition information:
-Calories: 177
-Total Fat: 5g
-Sodium: 796mg
-Total Carbohydrate: 26g
-Protein: 5g

77. Spanakopita Triangles

Spanakopita Triangles are a delicious Greek snack filled with spinach, feta cheese, and herbs, all wrapped up in layers of filo pastry.
Serving: Makes 24 spanakopita triangles.
Preparation Time: 15 minutes
Ready Time: 45 minutes

Ingredients:

-380g spinach
-1 small red onion, finely chopped
-4 tablespoons olive oil, plus extra for brushing
-3 spring onions, sliced
-225g feta cheese, crumbled
-2 large eggs
-125ml milk
-1 teaspoon ground nutmeg
-1/2 teaspoon salt
-30g fresh dill, chopped
-18 sheets filo pastry

Instructions:
1. Preheat the oven to 375°F (190°C).
2. In a large bowl, combine the spinach, red onion, olive oil, spring onions, feta, eggs, milk, nutmeg, salt and dill. Stir well to combine.
3. Take one sheet of filo pastry and brush with olive oil. Place another sheet of filo on top. Spoon 2-3 tablespoons of the spinach mixture onto the centre of the pastry and fold the pastry up into a triangle shape. Repeat this process with the remaining filo and spinach mixture.
4. Place the spanakopita triangles on a lined baking tray and brush them with olive oil.
5. Bake for 30-35 minutes, until golden brown.

Nutrition information: (Per Serving)
Calories – 160kcal
Fat – 9.8 g
Carbohydrates – 11.2 g
Protein – 6.3 g

78. Armenian Dolma

Armenian Dolma is a traditional dish of the Mediterranean made primarily with vine leaves, rice, and various spices. This delicious dish is simple to make and can be served as an appetizer or a part of the main course.
Serving: Serves 6
Preparation Time: 30 minutes

Ready Time: 1 hour 30 minutes

Ingredients:
- 1 tablespoon olive oil
- 1 onion, diced
- 2 cloves garlic, minced
- 1 teaspoon ground cumin
- 2 tablespoons tomato paste
- 1/4 teaspoon pepper
- 2 tablespoons fresh parsley, chopped
- 1/4 cup uncooked long grain white rice
- 1/2 cup crumbled feta cheese
- 1/2 cup raisins
- 8 vine leaves
- 2 tablespoons butter

Instructions:
1. Heat oil in a large saucepan over medium-high heat. Add onion and garlic and sauté, stirring often, until tender, about 5 minutes.
2. Reduce heat to low. Add cumin, tomato paste, pepper, parsley, rice, feta, and raisins. Mix well and cook for 5 minutes.
3. Place one vine leaf on a clean work surface with the stem end facing you. Place a spoonful of the mixture in the center of the leaf and fold the edges over the filling. Repeat with remaining leaves.
4. Place the stuffed vine leaves in a large skillet. Drizzle with butter and pour in enough water to cover the bottom of the skillet.
5. Cover the skillet and bring to a boil. Lower heat to a simmer and cook for 40 minutes.

Nutrition information:
Calories: 118, Total Fat: 5 g, Saturated Fat: 2 g, Trans Fat: 0 g, Sodium: 93 mg, Total Carbohydrates: 17 g, Dietary Fiber: 2 g, Sugars: 7 g, Protein: 3 g

79. Tuna Salad with Olives

This tuna salad with olives is a quick and easy dish that you can prepare in less than 15 minutes. Perfect for picnics, lunchboxes or as a light evening meal.

Serving: 2

Preparation time: 10 minutes

Ready time: 15 minutes

Ingredients:
- 2 cans (7-8 oz each) tuna
- 1/2 cup mayonnaise
- 1/4 cup diced olives
- 2 tablespoons dijon mustard
- 2 tablespoons chopped fresh parsley
- 1/4 teaspoon garlic powder
- Salt and pepper to taste

Instructions:
1. Drain and flake the tuna into a large bowl.
2. Add mayonnaise, olives, dijon mustard, parsley, garlic powder, salt, and pepper.
3. Stir until all Ingredients are combined and the tuna is coated.
4. Refrigerate for 30 minutes before serving.

Nutrition information:
Calories: 297, Fat: 20g, Carbohydrates: 5g, Protein: 25g, Sodium: 571mg

80. Sephardic Saffron Rice

Sephardic Saffron Rice is a delicious, fragrant, and savory dish made with short grain rice, saffron, chicken broth, and typically other flavorful Ingredients.

Serving: 4

Preparation Time: 15 minutes

Ready Time: 35 minutes

Ingredients:
- 2 tablespoons olive oil
- 2 cloves garlic, minced

- 1 1/2 cups short grain rice
- 2 teaspoons ground turmeric
- 4 cups chicken broth
- 1/4 teaspoon saffron threads
- 1 teaspoon ground cumin
- 2 tablespoons chopped fresh parsley

Instructions:
1. Heat the olive oil in a large saucepan over medium heat.
2. Stir in the garlic and cook for 1 minute.
3. Stir in the rice and turmeric and cook for another minute.
4. Pour in the chicken broth and bring to a boil.
5. Add the saffron threads, cumin, and parsley and stir to combine.
6. Cover the pot with a lid and reduce heat to low.
7. Simmer for 25 minutes or until the rice is tender.
8. Remove from heat and serve.

Nutrition information: Per Serving size of 1 cup: 361 calories, 12g fat, 52g carbohydrates, 6g protein

81. Algerian Brik

Algerian Brik is an incredibly flavorful Algerian pastry dish. It features a light, crunchy outer shell filled with a tasty combination of sautéed onion, egg, and parsley. This popular dish can be served as an appetizer or main course.
Serving: 4
Preparation Time: 20 minutes
Ready Time: 40 minutes

Ingredients:
- 2 tablespoons olive oil
- 1 large onion, chopped
- 1 clove garlic, minced
- 1 teaspoon ground cumin
- 1/4 teaspoon red pepper flakes
- 1/4 cup flat-leaf parsley, chopped
- 4 large eggs

- 4 sheets brick pastry dough
- 1/2 cup feta cheese, crumbled or grated
- Salt and pepper to taste

Instructions:
1. Heat olive oil in a large skillet over medium heat. Add the onions and garlic and sauté until the onions are soft and translucent, about 10 minutes.
2. Add the cumin, red pepper flakes, and parsley and stir to combine. Remove from the heat and allow to cool.
3. Once cooled, crack one egg into a bowl and add to the onion mixture. Stir to combine.
4. Unfold the brick pastry dough and cut into four pieces. Place about 1/4 cup of the egg mixture on one side of the pastry dough. Fold the dough over and crimp the edges with a fork to seal.
5. Heat a large skillet over medium heat. Place the brik into the skillet and cook until the pastry is golden brown and crunchy. Flip and cook on the other side.
6. Remove from heat and top with crumbled or grated feta cheese. Serve warm.

Nutrition information: Calories: 207 kcal, Carbohydrates: 12 g, Protein: 8 g, Fat: 14 g, Saturated Fat: 4 g, Cholesterol: 97 mg, Sodium: 357 mg, Potassium: 108 mg, Fiber: 1 g, Sugar: 1 g, Vitamin A: 572 IU, Vitamin C: 8 mg, Calcium: 79 mg, Iron: 1 mg

82. Dolmas

Dolmas are tasty, vegan and vegetarian friendly stuffed grape leaves that can be served as an appetizer or meal. They are easy to make and full of flavor, making them a great dish for any occasion.
Serving: Makes 12 Dolmas
Preparation time: 20 minutes
Ready Time: 20-25 minutes

Ingredients:
• 12 large grape leaves
• 1/3 cup long grain white rice

- 1/2 cup chopped onion
- 1/2 cup chopped parsley
- 1/2 teaspoon ground coriander seed
- Sea salt and black pepper, to taste
- 1/4 cup olive oil
- 1/4 cup freshly squeezed lemon juice
- 1/4 cup water

Instructions:
1. Rinse the grape leaves and remove the stems.
2. In a medium bowl, mix together the rice, onion, parsley, coriander, salt, and pepper.
3. Take one grape leaf and place it on a plate, shiny side down. Place about 1 tablespoon of the rice mixture into the center of the leaf.
4. Fold the sides of the leaf over to enclose the rice mixture and roll up the leaf from the stem end.
5. Repeat with the remaining leaves and rice mixture.
6. Place the rolled grape leaves in a large pot or deep skillet.
7. In a small bowl, whisk together the olive oil, lemon juice, and water. Pour this mixture over the grape leaves and bring to a low simmer.
8. Cover and simmer for 20-25 minutes, or until the rice is cooked through.
9. Serve warm or at room temperature.

Nutrition information
Per Serving: 114 calories; 6.9 g fat; 9.7 g carbohydrates; 2.3 g protein; 0.6 g fiber

83. Turkish Karnıyarık

Turkish Karnıyarık is a savory eggplant dish from the Turkish cuisine that is filled with a delicious seasoned beef and onion stuffing.
Serving: This recipe makes 4 servings.
Preparation time: 30 minutes
Ready Time: 30 minutes

Ingredients:
- 2 large eggplants
- 4 tablespoons olive oil

- 1 onion, chopped
- 4 ounces ground beef
- 1 garlic clove, finely chopped
- 1 teaspoon ground cumin
- 1 teaspoon paprika
- salt and pepper to taste
- 4 tablespoons chopped fresh parsley

Instructions:
1. Preheat oven to 425°F (220°C).
2. Cut the eggplants lengthwise, scoop out the flesh, and reserve shells.
3. Heat 2 tablespoons of olive oil in a skillet over medium heat and sauté the onions until transparency.
4. Add the ground beef and garlic and cook until the beef is no longer pink.
5. Add cumin, paprika, salt and pepper, and chopped parsley; stir to combine, and assist for a few minutes.
6. Oil the eggplants shells with the remaining olive oil and bake them in a preheated oven for about 10 minutes.
7. Remove from oven, and fill with the beef mixture.
8. Return the stuffed eggplants to the oven and bake for an additional 20 minutes.

Nutrition information
Per serving (1 stuffed eggplant):
Calories: 400kcal, Carbohydrates: 18g, Protein: 16g, Fat: 29g, Saturated Fat: 8g, Cholesterol: 58mg, Sodium: 256mg, Potassium: 541mg, Fiber: 5g, Sugar: 8g, Vitamin A: 600IU, Vitamin C: 7.2mg, Calcium: 43mg, Iron: 2.2mg

84. Feta and Olive Salad

This Feta and Olive Salad is a great summer side dish to accompany any meal. It is light, nutritious and takes just minutes to prepare.
Serving: 8 to 10
Preparation Time: 15 minutes
Ready Time: 15 minutes

Ingredients:
- 4 cups of mixed greens, such as romaine, baby spinach, rocket, etc
- ¼ cup of crumbled feta cheese
- 2 tablespoons of chopped fresh oregano
- 1/2 cup of pitted black olives
- 1/2 cup of pitted kalamata olives
- 2 tablespoons of extra-virgin olive oil
- 2 tablespoons of freshly squeezed lemon juice

Instructions:
1. Place the mixed greens in a large bowl.
2. Sprinkle the feta cheese, oregano, and olives over the top of the greens.
3. In a small bowl, whisk together the olive oil and lemon juice.
4. Drizzle the dressing over the salad, and toss to combine.

Nutrition information: Calories: 106; Fat: 9g; Saturated Fat: 2g; Cholesterol: 4mg; Sodium: 429mg; Carbohydrates: 3g; Fiber: 1g; Protein: 3g.

85. Algerian Shakshouka

Algerian Shakshouka is a tasty egg and tomato dish that is popular in North African cuisine. The dish is simple to make and has a medley of flavors. It makes a great breakfast, lunch, or dinner.
Serving: 4
Preparation time: 10 minutes
Ready time: 15 minutes

Ingredients:
• 2 tablespoons of olive oil
• 2 cloves garlic, minced
• 1 small onion, chopped
• 1 red pepper, chopped
• 1 teaspoon of cumin
• 1 teaspoon of paprika
• 1 teaspoon of coriander
• 1 can (14.5 oz) diced tomatoes

- Salt and pepper to taste
- 4 eggs

Instructions:

1. Preheat the oven to 375°F (190°C).
2. Heat the olive oil in a large skillet over medium heat. Add the garlic, onion, red pepper, cumin, paprika, and coriander. Stir and cook for 5 minutes until the vegetables are soft.
3. Add the diced tomatoes and cook for a few minutes until the tomatoes are cooked through.
4. Add salt and pepper to taste.
5. Gently crack the eggs into the skillet with the tomato mixture.
6. Transfer the skillet to the preheated oven and bake for 12 minutes until the eggs are cooked through.
7. Serve with warm crusty bread or couscous.

Nutrition information:

Serving Size: 1
Calories: 142
Total Fat: 8.3 g
Saturated Fat: 2.1 g
Cholesterol: 176 mg
Sodium: 196 mg
Carbohydrates: 7.2 g
Fiber: 1.9 g
Protein: 8.6 g

86. Greek Feta Dip

Greek Feta Dip is a classic Mediterranean dip full of flavor and a must-have for any get-together. This easy dip requires minimal Ingredients and only a few steps to make.
Serving: 10
Preparation Time: 10 minutes
Ready Time: 20 minutes

Ingredients:

- 8 ounces of crumbled feta cheese

- 1/4 cup of extra-virgin olive oil
- 1 clove of garlic, minced
- 1 teaspoon of fresh lemon juice
- 1 tablespoon of chopped fresh parsley
- Salt and pepper to taste

Instructions:
1. In a medium bowl, stir together feta cheese, olive oil, garlic, lemon juice, parsley, salt, and pepper until combined.
2. Cover and refrigerate for 10 minutes to allow the flavors to combine.
3. Serve Greek Feta Dip with pita bread, crackers, or vegetable slices for dipping.

Nutrition information (per serving):
Calories: 180
Fat: 15 g
Carbohydrates: 1 g
Protein: 9 g

87. Matbucha

Matbucha is a Moroccan staple; a cooked tomato and pepper salad that is full of flavor and very healthy. It's a mix of cooked cleaned tomatoes and peppers cooked with garlic, spices, and olive oil. It can be served as a meal or side dish and pairs very well with couscous or bread.
Serving: 4
Preparation Time: 5 minutes
Ready Time: 25 minutes

Ingredients:
- 4 large tomatoes, cleaned and cubed
- 1 green bell pepper, cleaned
- 1 red bell pepper, cleaned
- 4 large cloves of garlic, minced
- 2 tablespoons of olive oil
- 1 teaspoon cumin
- 1 teaspoon paprika
- 1 teaspoon cayenne pepper

- Salt, to taste

Instructions:
1. Heat a large skillet over medium heat.
2. Add olive oil and minced garlic and sauté for 2-3 minutes.
3. Add the cubed tomatoes, green pepper, and red peppers and cook until the vegetables are soft and beginning to brown, about 10-15 minutes.
4. Add the cumin, paprika, cayenne pepper, and salt.
5. Cook for a few more minutes, stirring often, until the vegetables are soft and lightly browned.
6. Serve warm over couscous or with bread.

Nutrition information:
Serving Size: 1/4 of recipe
Calories: 73
Fat: 4.5 grams
Carbohydrates: 8.5 grams
Protein: 2.2 grams

88. Moroccan Chicken Pastilla

Moroccan Chicken Pastilla is a traditional dish with roots from the Andalusian cuisine. It is made of a mixture of sweet and savory flavors that are incredibly enjoyable. This delectable dish can be served either as a main meal or as a side dish.
Serving: 4
Preparation Time: 30 minutes
Ready Time: 1 hour 30 minutes

Ingredients:
- 14 ounces of boneless chicken
- 2 tablespoons of butter
- 1 teaspoon of cinnamon
  Salt and pepper to taste
- 1/2 cup of almond slices
- 5 tablespoons of blanched almonds
- 1/2 cup of cilantro chopped

- 2 tablespoons of olive oil
- 10 sheets of phyllo dough
- 1/4 cup of melted butter

Instructions:
1. Preheat the oven to 375°F.
2. In a large skillet over medium heat, add butter until melted.
3. Add the chicken, cinnamon, salt, and pepper and cook, stirring occasionally until chicken is fully cooked.
4. In a bowl, combine the almonds, cilantro, and olive oil.
5. Place a sheet of phyllo dough on a baking sheet.
6. Top with some of the almond mixture.
7. Drizzle with melted butter.
8. Top with another sheet of phyllo dough and repeat until all sheets are used.
9. Fold up the edges and brush with more melted butter.
10. Bake for 25 minutes, until golden brown.
11. Let cool before slicing and serving.

Nutrition information:
Calories: 394 kcal
Fat: 24.2 g
Carbohydrates: 18.7 g
Protein: 22.6 g

89. Egyptian Falafel

Egyptian Falafel is a savory and delicious deep fried chickpea fritter that is popular in Middle Eastern cuisine.
Serving: 4 servings
Preparation time: 10 minutes
Ready time: 35 minutes

Ingredients:
- 2 cans of chickpeas, drained and rinsed
- 2 tablespoons of fresh parsley, finely chopped
- 1 clove of garlic, minced
- 1 teaspoon of baking powder

- 1 teaspoon of ground cumin
- 1 teaspoon of ground coriander
- 1/2 teaspoon of ground cardamom
- 1 teaspoon of ground pepper
- 1 teaspoon of salt
- 1 teaspoon of olive oil
- 1/4 cup of all-purpose flour
- Oil for deep frying

Instructions:
1. Place the chickpeas in a large bowl and mash them with a fork until they are almost a paste.
2. Add the parsley, garlic, baking powder, cumin, coriander, cardamom, pepper, salt, and olive oil to the mashed chickpeas and mix together until everything is well combined.
3. Form the mixture into small balls, about the size of a ping-pong ball.
4. Heat oil over medium-high heat in a deep pot or pan.
5. Carefully drop the falafel balls into the hot oil and fry until golden brown, about 5 minutes.
6. Remove the falafel with a slotted spoon and place on a plate lined with paper towels to absorb the excess oil.
7. Serve warm.

Nutrition information: One serving of Egyptian Falafel contains approximately 157 calories, 6 grams of fat, 23 grams of carbohydrates, and 4 grams of protein.

90. Dolmades

Dolmades is an traditional Greek dish made of vine leaves stuffed with rice. It is both healthy and delicious and it usually served as an appetizer or as a side dish.
Serving: Makes 8-10 Dolmades
Preparation time: 10 minutes
Ready time: 1 hour 15 minutes

Ingredients:
• 8-10 vine leaves

- ½ cup of uncooked long grain white rice
- 1 onion, finely chopped
- 2 cloves of garlic, finely chopped
- 1 large tomato, peeled and finely chopped
- ½ teaspoon of ground cinnamon
- 1 teaspoon of ground allspice
- ¾ cup of olive oil
- ¾ cup of fresh parsley, finely chopped
- 1 tablespoon of fresh mint, finely chopped
- ¼ cup of pinenuts
- Juice from 1 lemon
- Salt, to taste

Instructions:
1. Preheat oven to 375°F.
2. Heat 2 tablespoons of olive oil in a medium saucepan. Sweat the onion and garlic over a medium heat for 5 minutes or until it starts to soften.
3. Add in the tomato, cinnamon, allspice and salt. Cook for another 5 minutes.
4. Add the uncooked rice and cook for 3 minutes, stirring constantly.
5. In a separate bowl, mix together the parsley, mint, pinenuts and remaining olive oil.
6. Gently lay the vine leaves in a shallow oven dish. Place 1 tablespoon of the rice mixture in the center of each leaf.
7. Fold the sides of the leaves in and fold the top and bottom over the filling.
8. Place the parcels, seam-side down, in the oven dish.
9. Pour the remaining olive oil mixture over the parcels.
10. Squeeze some lemon juice on top.
11. Bake for 45 minutes.

Nutrition information: 1 dolma contains 280 calories, 17.5 g fat, 5.2 g protein, 25 g carbohydrates, 4.5 g fiber, and 185 mg sodium.

91. Turkish Menemen

Turkish Menemen is a traditional dish made of sautéed tomatoes, eggs, onions, peppers, and spices. This easy-to-make breakfast dish makes for a flavorful and nutritious start to the day!

Serving: 4

Preparation time: 10 minutes

Ready time: 20 minutes

Ingredients:
- 2 tablespoons olive oil
- 1 onion, roughly chopped
- 2 green bell peppers, roughly chopped
- 2 garlic cloves, minced
- 2 tomatoes, roughly chopped
- Salt and pepper, to taste
- 4 eggs
- Chopped parsley, for garnish

Instructions:
1. Heat the olive oil in a large skillet over medium heat.
2. Add the chopped onions and bell peppers, and sauté until softened, about 6-7 minutes.
3. Add the garlic and tomatoes, and season with salt and pepper. Cook for about 5 minutes, stirring occasionally.
4. Crack the eggs over the vegetables, and stir to combine. Cover and cook until the eggs are set, about 6-7 minutes.
5. Serve hot with chopped parsley, if desired. Enjoy!

Nutrition information (per serving):
Calories: 236
Fat: 16g
Carbohydrates: 8g
Fiber: 2g
Protein: 14g

92. Greek Baklava

Greek Baklava is a classic dessert made up of multiple layers of filo pastry filled with chopped nuts and syrup and perfume with a hint of honey, cinnamon and cloves. This sweet comfort food is definitely a treat to behold.

Serving: This recipe serves around 10-12 people.

Preparation Time

15 minutes

Ready Time

50 minutes

Ingredients:

-700g Puff pastry
-Tablespoon of honey
-150ml of vegetable oil
-250g of walnuts
-200g of almonds
-2cups of water
-2 cups of sugar
-Juice from 1 lemon
-Cinnamon and cloves

Instructions:

1. Preheat oven to 180 degrees C.
2. Separate layers of puff pastry and spread each layer on a greased baking tray.
3. Combine walnuts and almonds in a bowl and lightly toast.
4. Mix together honey, vegetable oil, water, sugar, lemon juice and spices for the syrup.
5. Spread a layer of the nut mixture on top of the pastry.
6. Top with another pastry layer and repeat the process until all the pastry and nut mixture have been used.
7. Bake in preheated oven for around 40-50 minutes, or until golden brown.
8. Remove from oven and pour hot syrup over pastry.

Nutrition information

-Calories: 400
-Carbohydrates: 47g
-Protein: 9g
-Fat: 24g
-Fiber: 4g

93. Haroset Truffles

Haroset Truffles are an easy and delicious recipe that combines the classic Jewish holiday flavors of Haroset with rich, chocolatey truffle.
Serving: Makes 24 truffles
Preparation Time: 10 minutes
Ready Time: 1 hour

Ingredients:
- 1 cup unsalted peanuts
- 1 cup raisins
- 1/4 cup apple juice
- 1/4 cup honey
- 2 tablespoons date syrup
- 1 teaspoon ground cinnamon
- 2 tablespoons unsweetened cocoa powder
- 3 ounces semi-sweet chocolate, melted

Instructions:
1. In a food processor, pulse together the peanuts, raisins, apple juice, honey, date syrup, and cinnamon until a coarse paste forms.
2. Roll the mixture into 1-inch balls, then place on a parchment-lined baking sheet. Freeze for at least 1 hour.
3. Dip each truffle into the melted chocolate until fully coated. Place back on the baking sheet and freeze for 10 minutes.
4. Serve chilled or at room temperature.

Nutrition information: Per truffle - Calories: 72, Fat: 4 g, Cholesterol: 0 mg, Sodium: 0 mg, Carbohydrates: 9 g, Fiber: 2 g, Protein: 2 g

94. Sephardic Orange Cake

Sephardic orange cake is an exquisite Middle Eastern dessert packed with traditional flavors. With a unique combination of citrus, vanilla, and sugar, this cake will be a hit with family and friends alike. Serving: 8-10
Preparation Time: 10 minutes Ready Time: 1 hour

Ingredients:
- 4 large oranges
- 3 eggs
- 2 cups granulated sugar
- 2/3 cup vegetable oil
- 1 teaspoon vanilla extract
- 2 1/2 cups all-purpose flour
- 2 teaspoons baking powder
- 2 teaspoons cinnamon
- 1/2 teaspoon salt

Instructions:
1. Preheat oven to 350F/175C. Grease a springform baking pan.
2. Juice two oranges. Peel and finely chop the remaining two oranges. Discard any seeds.
3. In a medium-sized bowl, whisk the eggs, sugar, oil, orange juice, vanilla extract, and chopped oranges until smooth.
4. In a separate large bowl, combine the flour, baking powder, cinnamon, and salt.
5. Add the egg mixture to the flour mixture and stir until fully combined.
6. Pour the batter into the prepared baking pan and bake for 45-50 minutes or until a tester inserted into the center comes out clean.
7. Allow the cake to cool before unlocking the springform pan and serving.

Nutrition information: Per serving: 310 calories; 12.6 g fat; 45.3 g carbohydrates; 4.2 g protein; 83 mg cholesterol; 134 mg sodium.

95. Sephardic Stuffed Zucchini

These Sephardic Stuffed Zucchini are bursting with flavor and sure to impress even the pickiest of eaters. Combining the flavors of ground beef, rice, and garlic, this Mediterranean-style dish is a simple and delicious way to get dinner on the table.
Serving: Serves 4-6
Preparation time: 15 minutes
Ready time: 1 hour

Ingredients:

- 4 large zucchini
- 1 tsp olive oil
- 1 lb ground beef
- 1/2 cup cooked white rice
- 1 small onion, chopped
- 2 cloves garlic, minced
- Salt and pepper, to taste
- 2 eggs, beaten
- 1/4 cup fresh parsley, chopped
- 2 tablespoons toasted pine nuts
- 1/2 cup freshly grated Parmesan cheese, plus more for topping

Instructions:

1. Preheat oven to 375°F. Cut zucchini in half lengthwise and scoop out center of each half, reserving scooped out zucchini pulp for later. Place hollowed-out zucchini shells on baking sheet and brush outsides with olive oil. Bake for 20 minutes.

2. Meanwhile, heat large skillet over medium-high heat. Add ground beef and cook until browned, about 5 minutes. Drain fat, then add rice, onion, and garlic. Season with salt and pepper, to taste. Cook, stirring occasionally, for another 5 minutes. Remove from heat and let cool.

3. In a medium bowl, combine cooled beef mixture, reserved zucchini pulp, beaten eggs, parsley, pine nuts, and Parmesan cheese. Stir until well combined.

4. Divide mixture evenly between zucchini shells, pressing into shells. Bake for an additional 20-25 minutes, or until golden brown.

Nutrition information: Calories: 371, Total Fat: 12g, Saturated Fat: 4g, Cholesterol: 97mg, Sodium: 202mg, Carbohydrates: 34g, Fiber: 6g, Sugar: 4g, Protein: 30g

96. Pita Bread

Pita bread is a type of round, unleavened flatbread made with wheat flour. Its traditional shape is ideal for stuffing with various types of fillings to make sandwiches.

Serving: 4 people
Preparation Time: 10 minutes
Ready Time: 30 minutes

Ingredients:
-2 cups of all-purpose flour -1 teaspoon of baking powder -½ teaspoon of salt -1 teaspoon of sugar -1 teaspoon of olive oil -¾ cups of warm water

Instructions:
1. Preheat the oven to 425°F (220°C).
2. In a bowl, mix flour, baking powder, and salt.
3. Add in sugar and olive oil, and mix until combined.
4. Gradually add warm water and mix until a soft dough forms.
5. Turn the dough out onto a lightly floured surface and knead for about 5 minutes.
6. Cut the dough into 4 pieces and roll them into 10-inch circles.
7. Place the circles on a greased baking sheet.
8. Bake for 12 to 15 minutes, or until golden brown.
9. Remove from the oven and let cool before serving.

Nutrition information: Per serving (1 pita): 200 calories, 4.3g fat, 35g carbohydrates, 4g protein.

97. Almond and Olive Oil Cake

This Almond and Olive Oil Cake is a moist, delicious and healthier cake with a subtle, sweet flavor.
Serving: 6
Preparation Time: 15 minutes
Ready Time: 40 minutes

Ingredients:
- 1/2 cup blanched almond flour
- 3/4 cup all-purpose flour
- 1/2 teaspoon baking powder
- 1/4 teaspoon fine salt
- 5 large eggs

- 1/2 cup extra-virgin olive oil
- 3/4 cup honey
- Zest of 1 lemon
- 1/2 teaspoon fruit juice

Instructions:
1. Preheat oven to 350°F. Grease a 9-inch round cake pan with butter.
2. In a bowl, whisk together almond flour, all-purpose flour, baking powder, and salt.
3. In a separate bowl, whisk the eggs until light and airy. Whisk in olive oil, honey, lemon zest, and fruit juice.
4. Gradually add the dry Ingredients to the wet Ingredients until fully incorporated.
5. Pour the batter into the greased cake pan and bake for 25-30 minutes, or until a toothpick inserted into the center comes out clean.
6. Allow cake to cool before serving.

Nutrition information: Per serving: 304 calories, 20g fat, 29g carbs, 3g protein.

98. Bulgarian Banitsa

Bulgarian Banitsa is a popular pastry dish made with filo pastry, feta cheese, and eggs. It is a great breakfast or brunch option that can be customized to your taste preferences.
Serving: 6-8
Preparation Time: 20 minutes
Ready Time: 40 minutes

Ingredients:
- 2 cups feta cheese
- 8 ounces filo dough
- 5 eggs
- 1 cup butter, melted
- 2 tablespoon fresh parsley, chopped
- Salt and pepper to taste

Instructions:

1. Preheat oven to 350 degrees F.
2. In a bowl, mix together feta cheese, eggs, melted butter, parsley, salt, and pepper.
3. Lay out sheets of filo dough on a flat surface. Grease a baking dish with butter, and layer 5–6 sheets of filo dough in the bottom of the dish.
4. Spread the cheese mixture over the filo layers.
5. Take remaining filo dough sheets, and layer them over the cheese mixture.
6. Brush the top layer of pastry with melted butter, and sprinkle with parsley.
7. Bake in the preheated oven for 40 minutes, or until top layer is golden brown.

Nutrition information: per serving (8 servings)
Calories: 336
Fat: 23.8 g
Carbohydrates: 18.9 g
Protein: 11.3 g
Sodium: 590 mg

99. Carrot and Raisin Salad

Carrot and Raisin Salad combines crunchy carrots with sweetness from the raisins and a flavorful dressing to make a tasty and easy salad.
Serving: 6
Preparation Time: 10 minutes
Ready Time: 10 minutes

Ingredients:
2 cups shredded carrots, 1/2 cup golden raisins, 2 tablespoons lemon juice, 2 teaspoons sugar, salt and freshly ground pepper to taste.

Instructions.
1. In a large bowl, combine the carrots, raisins, lemon juice, sugar, and salt and pepper.
2. Toss to combine.
3. Refrigerate for 10 minutes
4. Serve and enjoy.

**Nutrition information: Per serving: 144 Calories, 11g
Carbohydrates, 0.4g Fat, 1.7g Protein, 0.6g Fiber.**

100. Israeli Couscous Salad

This light and flavorful Israeli couscous salad is a great crowd pleaser and perfect for a summer cookout. The combination of vegetables, herbs, and Israeli couscous make this unique dish both healthy and delicious.
Serving: 6
Preparation Time: 15 minutes
Ready Time: 15 minutes

Ingredients:
•1 cup Israeli couscous
•3 tablespoons olive oil
•1/2 teaspoon garlic powder
•1/4 teaspoon paprika
•1/2 cup cucumber, diced
•1/2 cup red pepper, diced
•1/2 cup feta cheese, crumbled
•2 tablespoons fresh parsley, chopped
•2 tablespoons fresh basil, chopped
•3 tablespoons red wine vinegar
•2 tablespoons lemon juice
•Salt and pepper, to taste

Instructions:
1.Bring 2 cups of water to a boil in a medium pot. Add the Israeli couscous, reduce to a simmer and cook for 10-15 minutes, or until all the water is absorbed.
2.Once the couscous is cooked, remove from the heat and let cool.
3.Meanwhile, in a large bowl, whisk together the olive oil, garlic powder, paprika, red wine vinegar, and lemon juice.
4.Add in the cooked couscous, cucumber, red pepper, feta cheese, parsley, basil, and salt and pepper.
5.Mix well to combine and chill for at least 15 minutes before serving.

Nutrition information: One serving (1/6 of recipe) contains 330 calories, 15g fat, 40g carbohydrate, 12g protein, 2g fiber, 360mg sodium.

101. Greek Yogurt with Honey and Nuts

Greek Yogurt with Honey and Nuts is a sweet and nutritious snack that can be enjoyed for breakfast or as an afternoon pick-me-up. Loaded with crunchy nuts and sweet honey, this favorite treat is simple to make.
Serving: 2
Preparation Time: 5 mins
Ready Time: 10 mins

Ingredients:
- 2 cups of plain Greek Yogurt
- 2 tablespoons of honey
- 1/4 cup of chopped walnuts

Instructions:
1. In a medium bowl, mix together the Greek yogurt and honey.
2. Fold in the chopped walnuts until they are evenly distributed.
3. Transfer the mixture to two individual bowls and serve.

Nutrition information: Per serving, Greek Yogurt with Honey and Nuts contains around 200 calories, 12 grams of fat, 22 grams of carbohydrates, 1 gram of fiber, and 8 grams of protein.

CONCLUSION

This cookbook, Savoring Sephardic Cuisine: 101 Delectable Recipes, has provided readers with an overview of the history and culture behind Sephardic cuisine and a diverse selection of recipes that can be used to create delicious dishes. The book includes flavors and ingredients from multiple countries and provides both novice and experienced cooks with the opportunity to experiment with new flavors and create their own dishes. This book is sure to be a hit amongst both traditional and modern kitchens, as it offers a wealth of recipes that span both centuries-old traditions and modern techniques. The book also offers helpful tips for cooking and plating, as well as food substitution options for those who wish to create a vegetarian, dairy-free, or gluten-free meal. Sephardic cuisine is both delicious and unique, and this book is an excellent gateway to explore the flavor and culture that has been passed down through generations. With its combination of both classic and innovative recipes, Savoring Sephardic Cuisine: 101 Delectable Recipes is sure to please any palate.

Made in the USA
Las Vegas, NV
12 December 2023

82662312R00066